FLORIDA
Off the Beaten Path

"A pleasantly low-key guide to more than 1,000 lesser-known sites worth a detour. . . ."
— Robert Jenkins, *St. Petersburg Times*

"Authors Bill and Diana Gleasner have been enjoying Florida for more than thirty years and their intimate knowledge reflects virtually every corner of this popular winter state."
— Gordon Charles, syndicated travel writer

"Offers descriptions of unique attractions often missed by travelers to Florida."
— *Michigan Living*

"This book is . . . a good item to keep in the glove compartment so that it will be available during those all-important times when you're seeking an unplanned, spontaneous adventure. . . ."
— *Sunday Advocate, Vacation & Travel Special Edition,*
Baton Rouge

FLORIDA
Off the Beaten Path
Second Edition

by **Diana and Bill Gleasner**

A Voyager Book

The Globe Pequot Press

Chester, Connecticut

Library of Congress Cataloging-in-Publication Data

Gleasner, Diana C.
    Florida: Off the Beaten Path/Diana and Bill Gleasner — 2nd ed.
       p.   cm.
    "A Voyager book"
    ISBN 0-87106-481-2
    1. Florida—Description and travel—1981—Guide–books.
I. Gleasner, Bill. II Title.
F309.3.G55 1990
917.5904'63—dc20   90-32652
                                    CIP

Manufactured in the United States of America
Second Edition/First Printing

Cover Illustration by M. A. Dube.
Text Illustrations by Carol Drong.

Contents

To our friend and colleague
Bill Hensley

Introduction

Warning! Straying from the beaten interstate can be addictive. But is it ever fun!

By poking and prowling around this incredible state, we discovered a high rise for bats, the world's smallest police station, a McDonald's complete with salt licks and hitching posts, a museum dedicated to the inventor of air conditioning, and an Arctic blizzard (Eglin Air Force Base Climatic Laboratory).

Florida seems to have cornered the "world's largest" market. We saw the largest concentration of saw grass, the largest bald cypress tree and the largest collections of Frank Lloyd Wright buildings, Art Deco buildings, Salvador Dali art works and Tiffany glass in the world. We even strolled the world's longest continuous sidewalk.

We traveled by inner tube, pontoon boat, car, motorhome, houseboat, sailboat, seaplane, canoe, motorized gondola, and airboat. Our meanderings took us through Little Havana, the Greek community of Tarpon Springs and a Miccosukee Indian Village.

We heard a dolphin take a deep breath in the Everglades, toured a thoroughbred farm and chatted with a cow hunter rounding up one of the few remaining herds of scrub cattle in existence. We saw a tapir, manatees, wood storks, a herd of buffalo and alligators romping in the surf!

We slept in a lighthouse, cheered ourselves hoarse at a rodeo, hunted for fossil shark teeth, lunched in an indoor swimming pool (luckily for us, it was dry), nibbled on alligator tail (lucky for us, it was not connected to anyone) and pitched a tent on more than a few of the Ten Thousand Islands.

In short, we have enjoyed an abundance of serendipitous experiences. But there are many more discoveries waiting to be made in Florida. Write us (in care of The Globe Pequot Press, 138 West Main Street, Chester, CT 06412) and tell us your special finds.

Travel safely and have a terrific time!

P.S. Restaurant cost categories refer to the price of entrees without beverages, desserts, taxes or tips. Those listed as inexpensive are under $5, moderate prices range between $5 and $10 and expensive are over $10.

P.P.S. Here are a few addresses that will come in handy. We especially recommend sending for the state parks brochure so you can take advantage of one of the most marvelous state park systems in the country.

General Information
Florida Chamber of Commerce
P.O. Box 11309
Tallahassee, FL 32302
(904) 222-2831

Florida Division of Tourism
Visitor Inquiry
126 W. Van Buren Street
Tallahassee, FL 32399
(904) 487-1462

Festivals and Events
Department of Commerce
Division of Tourism
Collins Building
107 W. Gaines Street
Tallahassee, FL 32399

Historical Sites
Department of State
Division of Archives, History
and Records
The Capitol
Tallahassee, FL 32399
(904) 487-2333

State Parks
Florida Department of Natural
Resources
Division of Recreation and Parks
Bureau of Education and
Information
3900 Commonwealth Boulevard
Tallahassee, FL 32303
(904) 488-7326

The prices and rates listed in this guidebook were confirmed at press time. We recommend, however, that you call establishments before traveling to obtain current information.

Off the Beaten Path in Northeast Florida

1–8   Amelia Island

9–16   Jacksonville Area

Gainesville Area

30
29

26–28   24
25   St. Augustine Area

17–22

23

1. Centre Street Fernandina
2. Palace Saloon
3. San Carlos Winery
4. Bailey House
5. Fort Clinch State Park
6. Seahorse Stable
7. Lighthouse lodging
8. Amelia Island Plantation
9. Little Talbot Island State Park
10. Kingsley Plantation
11. U.S. Naval Station
12. Fort Caroline National Memorial
13. Riverwalk
14. Museum of Science and History
15. Alexander Brest Planetarium
16. Cummer Gallery of Art
17. Castillo de San Marcos
18. St. George Street
19. Spanish Quarter
20. Lightner Museum
21. Cafe Alcazar
22. Capt. Jim's Conch House Restaurant
23. Bulow Plantation Ruins Historic Site
24. Palatka Ravine State Ornamental Garden
25. Marjorie Kinnan Rawlings State Historic Site
26. Payne's Prairie State Preserve
27. Florida Museum of Natural History
28. Devil's Millhopper State Geological Site
29. O'Leno State Park
30. Ichetucknee Springs State Park

Northeast Florida

Amelia Island

Amelia Island, with its 13 miles of uncrowded sandy beaches, has already been discovered. In fact, it is the onlyUnited States location to have been under eight different flags: French, Spanish, British, American Patriots (1812), Green Cross of Florida (1817), Mexican, Confederate and United States.

The Timucuan Indians' simple life was disrupted first by the French in the sixteenth century and then by the Spanish. The Union Jack was raised in 1763, but the Tories who converged on the island during the Revolutionary War left when Florida was ceded to Spain. A military adventurer, General Sir Gregor MacGregor, captured the island and claimed it as his for a brief time, but was ousted by a pirate who took over ostensibly for Mexico. After the United States government took formal possession, the claim was disputed by the Confederacy, which raised its flag here during the Civil War.

Federal occupation during the Civil War triggered a tourist boom. This, with an impressive flow of money created by the shipping business, made Fernandina Beach a prosperous community. Before long, handsome Victorian homes lined the residential streets. These architectural gems, dating from 1857 and ranging from old steamboat gothic to Queen Anne style, earned the 30-block Old Town district, also known as **Centre Street Fernandina,** a listing on the National Register of Historic Places. Be sure to stop at the Chamber of Commerce near the city docks for walking or driving tour directions to this gingerbread seaport.

It was from these docks that the country's first offshore shrimp trawlers sailed out early in this century. For a look at the multicolored shrimp nets being made at Burbank's Net Factory, go through the back door of Standard Marine Supply Corporation on Alachua Street. This father-son operation does not offer a formal tour, but keep in mind that Fernandina Beach is the only town in the country that has a shrimp net manufacturer on site to accommodate the fleet. Be sure to be at the docks at sunset to watch the shrimping fleet return with the day's catch.

Stroll past the old **Palace Saloon,** or better yet, stop in to inspect its splendid carved mahogany bar, which a reliable source has called "the best bar east of Boise." Be sure to sam-

Palace Saloon

ple a miniplatter of fresh boiled shrimp while enjoying local color in the oldest saloon in Florida. The Palace Saloon is on the corner of Second and Centre; (904) 261–9068.

Historic Centre Street bristles with fascinating shops and boutiques. The Ships Lantern (210 Centre Street) offers a fine selection of paintings, prints, woodcarvings, scrimshaw and jewelry made from shark teeth found in the area. For designer wicker and rattan furniture, Italian pottery and Dhurrie rugs, try the Southern Traveler at 213 Centre Street.

If you're fresh out of chocolate fettucine or just want to stock up on rose geranium jelly and marinated asparagus, the Cross-Eyed Bear (201 Centre Street) is the place to satisfy your gourmet cravings.

C House Colony (Beech and S. Eighth streets) offers a variety of diversions for the shopper ranging from shells, sportswear, Christmas decorations, and kitchenware to fine crystal. Charlotte's (a European cafe) specializes in exquisite desserts. The building is an 1889 treasure; note the Chinese Chippendale influence on the front porch. Open Monday through Saturday 10:00 A.M.—5:30 P.M.

James Gildenston's wife, Karen, told him to give up his hobby or get it out of the house. So this podiatrist became a winemaker. (Please muzzle your grape stomping jokes; he's heard them all.) **San Carlos Winery** uses Muscadine grapes, the same variety early European settlers found growing wild in Florida, to produce its fruity red and white wines. This is a very small operation, but you're welcome to take a free tour and sample the product of Florida's newest winery. Located a couple blocks off Centre Street at 112 S. Third Street in Fernandina Beach's historic district. The winery is open noon—5:00 P.M. Monday through Saturday; (904) 277–3236.

Even if you don't stay in the **Bailey House,** be sure to take a good look at this 1895 Victorian bed and breakfast inn in the heart of the historic district. Its turrets, gables, bays, fishscale decoration and stained glass windows make it a showcase. No wonder it cost $10,000—an outrageous amount in 1895! The rooms are filled with carved furniture, brass beds, pump organs, fringed lamps and footed bathtubs, and guests are served a continental breakfast in the elegant dining room. No children, pets or smoking in

4

the building. Located at 28 Seventh Street, the Bailey House address is P.O. Box 805, Fernandina Beach, FL 32034; (904) 261–5390.

Fort Clinch State Park on Atlantic Avenue in Fernandina Beach welcomes visitors to the most northeasterly point in Florida. Its European-style brick masonry is unique in this country, and you'll get a splendid view of the Atlantic Ocean and Georgia's Cumberland Island from the fort's ramparts. On the first full weekend of every month, rangers reenact

Bailey House

the 1864 occupation in full period costume. The park's recreation facilities include saltwater fishing (1,500-foot lighted pier), swimming, camping, picnicking and hiking. The park, which is on Atlantic Avenue in Fernandina Beach (off SR A1A), opens at 8:00 A.M. and closes at sunset year-round. Fort Clinch State Park, 2601 Atlantic Avenue, Fernandina Beach, FL 32034; (904) 261–4212.

Amelia Island is one of the last spots on the Atlantic seaboard where you can ride horseback on the beach. Rides go out daily, weather permitting, and last approximately one and a quarter hours. Inexperienced riders should not hesitate; **Seahorse Stable** has a gentle horse for you. The stable is located on SR A1A at the south end of the island. For reservations, call (904) 261–4878.

If you've always wanted to stay in a **lighthouse** right on the beach, this is your chance. Four floors include two bedrooms (sleeps up to six), two baths, a kitchen and dining area and an observation deck for expansive viewing of the great Atlantic Ocean. Wallpapered in nautical charts, this is the place for faraway dreams. Breakfast and the morning paper are delivered to your door. The lighthouse is on the ocean side of SR A1A on the northern end of Amelia Island. Write to Amelia Island Lodging Systems, 584 South Fletcher, Amelia Island, FL 32034; (904) 261–4148.

Amelia Island Plantation is a low-key four-star resort offering a wide range of accommodations and amenities ranging from a beautiful beach and complete health club to a well-supervised children's program. Tennis enthusiasts have the run of twenty-five courts at Plantation Racket Club, and golfers play on twenty-seven challenging holes, which architect Pete Dye claims are the only true links on the East Coast. The fishing is fine whether it's deep-sea tarpon and kingfish charter, freshwater lagoon angling or crabbing.

Nature lovers should follow the Plantation's Sunken Forest Trail. The dense semitropical growth includes palms, magnolias and live oaks festooned with Spanish moss. About a quarter of this resort community has been set aside as a nature preserve enjoyed by raccoons, opossums, armadillos and alligators.

Amelia Island Plantation's Pool Villas provide the last word on romantic getaways. Imagine rolling out of bed and into your own private indoor swimming pool in a villa hidden deep in a moss-draped forest. Add a nearby beach and candlelight dinners overlooking the ocean, and you have the ingredients of a perfect lovers' retreat. The Plantation is on the southern end of Amelia Island off U.S. A1A, 29 miles northeast of Jacksonville International Airport. Amelia Island Plantation, Amelia Island, FL 32034; 1–800–874–6878.

Jacksonville Area

Little Talbot Island State Park embraces a quiet curving beach hidden beyond the dunes and framed by graceful sea oats. This is a delightful spot to camp, swim and picnic on an unspoiled beach. Open 8:00 A.M. to sunset year-round. Little Talbot Island is 17 miles northeast of Jacksonville, off SR A1A; (904) 251–3231.

The house at **Kingsley Plantation,** believed to be the oldest plantation house in Florida, has been restored and furnished in pre–Civil War style. Long rows of crumbling slave quarters are a mute reminder of the days when Zephaniah Kingsley trained slaves for specialized tasks. Guided tours of the house are given daily at 9:30 A.M., 11:00 A.M., 1:30 P.M. and 3:00 P.M. This state historic site is on Fort George Island, off SR A1A; (904) 251–3122.

The Marine Science Education Center welcomes visitors to a marine museum, wet lab (with some twenty different aquaria) and a collection of marine specimens including everything from giant clam shells to huge whale vertebrae. The center, in the historic village of Mayport, is one block south of the ferry slip on SR A1A (1347 Palmer Street). The reason the center looks like a school is because it is one. Although this resource is primarily for students, visitors are welcome 8:00 A.M.—3:00 P.M. Monday through Friday except school holidays; (904) 246–2733.

U.S. Naval Station (on Mayport Road) at Mayport is home port for giant aircraft carriers as well as many smaller ships. Tours are given on weekends. Ask at the gate for ship location or phone Public Affairs Officer at (904) 246–5226. For information-packed pre-recorded message, call (904) 241–NAVY.

Fort Caroline National Memorial commemorates the

7

only French attempt to establish a colony in Florida (1564). The 138-acre park features exhibits, guided tours and an interpretive model of the original fort. The story told is a tragic one ending in the massacre of most of the French settlers by the Spanish from St. Augustine. Located about 5 miles from the mouth of the St. Johns River. Open daily 9:00 A.M.—5:00 P.M. Fort Caroline National Memorial, 12713 Fort Caroline Road, Jacksonville, FL 32225; (904) 641–7155. Free.

Jacksonville is Florida's largest and most populous city as well as its leading financial, industrial, transportation and commercial center. Situated on a bend in the St. Johns River, this bustling and prosperous port is a skyscrapered showcase of sophisticated urban amenities. The St. Johns, the only major river in the United States to flow from south to north, has been the focus of the city's development since Jacksonville was founded in 1822. An ambitious riverfront beautification program has recently spiffed up the south bank with its attractive **Riverwalk.** Be sure to stroll the boardwalk and enjoy a fine view of this bustling city.

Adjacent to the Riverwalk are several fine restaurants, an excellent museum and one of the world's tallest fountains, which erupts after dark into a spirited rainbow of colors. The **Museum of Science and History** is a treasure house of exploration for the whole family. Attractions include a 28-foot dinosaur skeleton, an exhibit of Florida Indian culture and the **Alexander Brest Planetarium** with its daily multimedia productions. The museum is on Gulf Life Drive at S. Main Street in Jacksonville. Open Mon-day—Thursday 10:00 A.M.—5:00 P.M., Friday and Saturday 10:00 A.M. to 10:00 P.M. and Sunday noon—5:00 P.M.; (904) 396–7062.

How grand to be able to promenade the Riverwalk, explore the museum and then satisfy your appetite in style. Crawdaddy's looks like a disaster from the outside, but that's part of its charm. The front yard of this ramshackle fish camp shanty features rusting skeletons of old cars, a rooster and chickens. Beneath the corrugated tin roof you'll find a fine restaurant. Try an appetizer of Florida alligator chased by beer cheese soup, cajun chicken and turtle pie. Crawdaddy's is at 1643 Prudential Drive, Jacksonville. Most dinner entrees range from moderate to expensive; (904) 396–3546.

The **Cummer Gallery of Art** features sculpture in a lovely formal garden setting, a permanent collection of Old Masters and a 720-piece collection of early Meissen Porcelain at 829 Riverside Avenue, Jacksonville. Open Tuesday through Friday 10:00 A.M.—4:00 P.M., Saturday noon—5:00 P.M. and Sunday 2:00—5:00 P.M. (904) 356–6857. Free.

The brewmaster's art is on display at the Anheuser-Busch Brewery. After your tour, enjoy a free taste of the product in the hospitality room. Take I-95 north to the Busch Drive exit. The brewery is at 111 Busch Drive, Jacksonville. Self-guiding and conducted tours are available 10:00 A.M.—5:00 P.M. Monday through Saturday; (904) 751–0700. Free.

Ever dream of chocolate? Peterbrooke Chocolatier has the answer to your dreams. The store overflows with chocolate tennis rackets, golf balls, teddy bears, even a chocolate record that can be inscribed with a message of your choice. The candy is made from a secret recipe (known only to three people), and you may view the hand dipping on the premises.

The specialty here is fresh creme truffles, but you may also indulge yourself in chocolate smothered oreos, fresh strawberries dipped in chocolate, or ice cream appropriately named Total Decadence (loaded with milk chocolate, semisweet chocolate and macadamia nuts).

The chocolatier ships his products all over the world but maintains a keen interest in the local community. Peterbrooke was the inspiration for much of the impressive restoration of the San Marco area, and you will want to visit other shops and restaurants in the area. (Nearby Cafe Carmon's desserts are made with this famous chocolate. Try the truffle cake.) Peterbrooke is at 2024 San Marco Boulevard, Jacksonville, FL 32207; (904) 398–2488.

Harriet Beecher Stowe's winter home is a delightful drive south from Jacksonville to the riverside village of Mandarin via SR 13 (San Jose Boulevard). You can't enter the home of the famous author of *Uncle Tom's Cabin,* but you can read the state historic marker that tells of her move to Florida to "plan for philanthropy among the Negroes." The Stowe family home and orange grove is at 12447 Mandarin Road, but you will find it more easily by looking for "Mandarin Community Club" and "Kate Monson's Well Baby Clinic" signs at the site.

St. Augustine Area

St. Augustine, 40 miles south of Jacksonville, is an important repository of history, not only for the community and the state but for the entire nation. In a cheerful, if sometimes unsettling mix, the city's carefully preserved past rubs shoulders with the most blatant commercialism, but it is impossible not to be impressed by the city's antiquity. A history that spans four centuries covers a lot of territory.

Ponce de Leon, landing in this general vicinity, claimed the region for Spain, but it was Pedro Menendez de Aviles, sent by the King of Spain to get rid of the French, who established the first settlement. Continuously occupied since 1565, St. Augustine was founded forty-two years before the colony at Jamestown and fifty-five years before the ocean-weary Pilgrims set foot on Plymouth Rock! Two highly recommended movies—*Dream of Empire* and *Struggle to Survive*—bring this dramatic story to life. The theatre is one block from the city gates at 5 Cordova Street. The films are shown 9:30 A.M.—5:30 P.M. daily; (904) 824–0339.

Imposing **Castillo de San Marcos** is well worth a visit. The King of Spain spent $30 million on this fort, which took nearly a quarter century to build. Overlooking Matanzas Bay, this national monument withstood many a siege but was never captured. Park rangers in Spanish uniforms provide plenty of smoke as well as action with their demonstrations of old-time firearms. Castillo de San Marcos National Monument, 1 Castillo Drive, St. Augustine. Open 8:30 A.M.—5:15 P.M. from end of October to end of April, 9:00 A.M.—5:45 P.M. the rest of the year; (904) 829–6506.

A faithful reconstruction of the 1750–1845 period centers on **St. George Street.** To absorb the Old World atmosphere, take a leisurely stroll by coquina-stone houses with overhanging balconies and walled garden patios that line the narrow streets. Be sure to visit the exquisite St. Photios National Greek Orthodox Shrine at 41 St. George Street. (Open 9:00 A.M.—5:00 P.M.) Attractive shops and restaurants lure visitors. You'll want to browse the Ancient Mariner gift shop and follow your nose to the Spanish Bakery. Ask for Spanish meat turnovers, better known as empanadas, to eat in the picnic area. (The bakery is open

9:00 A.M.—3:00 P.M.) The historic area is immediately south of the old city gate.

Don't miss the **Spanish Quarter** in the restoration area. Here the daily lives of soldiers and settlers are recreated by costumed guides and craftspeople who welcome your questions. Look for the red and white Spanish flag and enter at the Triay Orientation Center on St. George Street. Operated by the state, this quality attraction is open 9:00 A.M.—5:00 P.M. daily. Information and ticket window at the Triay House, St. George Street, St. Augustine; (904) 825–6830.

St. Augustine experienced its first tourism boom at the turn of the century, thanks to Henry Flagler. Impressed with the city's possibilities, he linked St. Augustine and Jacksonville by railroad. While he was at it, Flagler turned the town into a fashionable resort by building two grand hotels, the Ponce de Leon and the Alcazar. Visitors should not leave the city without at least a look at these two lavish hotels, their gardens and fountains. The Ponce de Leon serves as Flagler College (no charge to roam the campus), and the restored Alcazar houses the **Lightner Museum** with its three floors of fascinating collections. Open 9:00 A.M.—5:00 P.M. daily; (904) 824–2874. Both are at Cordova and King streets, St. Augustine.

What better spot to lunch than in the indoor swimming pool (fortunately it was drained some time ago) of the fantastic Alcazar Hotel (now the Lightner Museum). **Cafe Alcazar** is located in the rear of the museum right in the center of the Lightner Antique Mall. You may investigate the antique shops while waiting for a sandwich, salad or freshly baked quiche. Appropriately, considering the grand setting, the dozen tables are set with real flowers, linen tablecloths and china. Everything is tasty, especially the salad Alcazar and Alcazar ambrosia. Open 11:30 A.M.—2:30 P.M. Tuesday through Saturday and for brunch on Sunday 10:30 A.M.—2:00 P.M. Lunch prices are inexpensive; (904) 824–7813.

Imagine having dinner in your own private thatched hut overlooking the water at sunset. **Capt. Jim's Conch House Restaurant** is known for succulent seafood as well as an enchanting tropical atmosphere. This unusual restaurant is the brainchild of the Ponces, who are descended from the Solanas, believed to be the oldest documented family in the

11

Capt. Jim's Conch House Restaurant

United States. Family records on file in the Catholic Cathedral in St. Augustine date back to 1594.

The owners' interest in local history is evidenced in the extensive collection of nautical antiques used throughout the restaurant. The thatched roof, made of more than 8,000 palm fronds, is the work of the Ponce brothers and a Seminole Indian and his son.

The Conch House Restaurant steams its seafood entrees in special spices and sauces. Specialties of the house include conch chowder, conch fritters, stuffed clams and Capt. Jim's Steamed Clams. For dessert try almond amaretto mousse or chocolate truffle mousse.

You have your choice of dining on the outdoor deck, in a private dining pod or inside the Conch House Restaurant. Come by sea (free dockage while dining) or by land. After crossing the Bridge of Lions from the historic area of St. Augustine, take SR A1A South for 6 blocks, turn left at sign, go 2 1/2 blocks to 57 Comares Avenue, St. Augustine. Open Sunday through Thursday 11:30 A.M.—9:00 P.M. and Friday and Saturday 11:30 A.M.—10:00 P.M. Most dinner entrees range from moderate to expensive; (904) 824–2046.

Those seeking a spot to spend the night that is as charming as it is convenient should make reservations at The Kenwood Inn. This bed and breakfast hostelry (built between 1865 and 1886) is located within the Historic District between the Oldest House and the famous Castillo de San Marcos. Most of St. Augustine's historic sights and fine restaurants are within walking distance.

The fifteen rooms range in size from small and cozy to spacious; each has its own unique personality (choose Shaker, colonial or Victorian), and all have private baths. A small outdoor swimming pool is an appreciated extra, and innkeepers Mark and Kerrianne Constant make everyone (except small children and pets) feel warmly welcome. The Kenwood Inn, 38 Marine Street, St. Augustine, FL 32084; (904) 824-2116.

South of St. Augustine are sights in Bunnell and Palatka not to be missed. The **Bulow Plantation Ruins Historic Site** features an old sugar mill and the crumbling foundation of an ancient mansion destroyed during the Seminole Indian Wars. Guided tours are available. The ruins are southeast of Bunnell on Old Kings Road; (904) 439-2219.

If your thoughts turn to **Palatka Ravine State Ornamental Garden,** it's probably spring. During February and March, the azaleas and camellias are at their peak. You may drive the road that loops around the edges of three steep ravines, jog the popular exercise course or just stroll the paths thinking end-of-winter thoughts. One hundred thousand azaleas can't be wrong. A mile southeast of Palatka on Twigg Street (off Moseley Avenue); (904) 329-3721. Open daily 8:00 A.M. to sunset. Free.

Gainesville Area

Marjorie Kinnan Rawlings found inspiration in the backwater community of Cross Creek. This semitropical low country was the setting for her Pulitzer-prize winning novel, *The Yearling.* The author's rambling farmhouse, complete with old-fashioned canned goods on the kitchen shelves and her antique typewriter on the screened porch, looks as if she had just stepped out for a moment.

Rawlings quickly grew to love this place and its people, which she immortalized in her autobiographical book, *Cross Creek.* Her neighbors were "crackers," rural folk native to the region who were used to "making do." They made what living there was from the land, put on no airs and wore their southern heritage with pride. The author compiled a book of regional recipes titled *Cross Creek Cookery.* (The nearby Yearling Restaurant specializes in fried alligator tail and other local favorites.)

The **Marjorie Kinnan Rawlings State Historic Site** is in Cross Creek, off SR 325. Open every day (except Tuesday and Wednesday) 10:00—11:30 A.M. and 1:00—4:30 P.M. Tours are given every half-hour. Marjorie Kinnan Rawlings State Historic Site, Rte. 3, Box 92, Hawthorne, FL 32640; (904) 466–3672.

Florida's home where the buffalo roam is **Payne's Prairie State Preserve** just south of Gainesville. Indian artifacts have been unearthed here that date back to 7000 B.C. The Visitor Center contains interesting exhibits on the natural and cultural history of the preserve. (It was once a large Spanish cattle ranch.) A nearby observation tower provides a scenic overlook of this vast, marshy sea of grass.

The park offers boating (no gasoline-powered boats allowed), fishing and swimming in Lake Wauberg, as well as camping, birdwatching and horseback riding. (Bring your own horse.) The entrance is on U.S. 441, approximately 1 1/2 miles north of Micanopy. Open 8:00 A.M. to sunset year-round. Paynes Prairie State Preserve, Rte. 2, P.O. Box 41, Micanopy, FL 32667; (904) 466–3397.

The Wine and Cheese Gallery in Gainesville with umbrellaed tables in a shady courtyard is a fine spot for lunching. Go right on through the front of the Gallery—which is a deli and wine shop—and hang a left to reach the courtyard. In inclement weather, take a right to the inside dining room. As you might imagine, they offer a super selection of wines, or you may choose from more than a hundred kinds of imported beer. The sandwiches are a treat (they bake their own French bread), as are the salads. Try the Big Cheese, a fat sandwich consisting of Cream Havarti, Jarlsberg and Danish Caraway or a lettuce salad loaded with rare roast beef, fresh mushrooms and Fjordland Swiss. The Wine and Cheese Gallery is at 113 N. Main Street in Gainesville. Open 11:00 A.M.—2:15 P.M. Monday through Saturday; (904) 372–8446. Inexpensive to moderate.

Gainesville's outstanding **Florida Museum of Natural History** offers fascination for all ages with its replica of a Mayan palace and reconstructed Florida cave. The cave comes complete with cave critters, but don't worry, they don't fly. What a find! The museum is on the University of Florida campus at the corner of Newell Drive and Museum Road. Open Monday through Saturday 9:00 A.M.—5:00 P.M., Sunday and holidays 1:00—5:00 P.M. Admission and parking are free; call (904) 392-1721. The museum's Collectors Shop, open during museum hours, carries a fine selection of items relating to the natural and social sciences.

Just down the road from Florida State Museum is the lush Lake Alice Wildlife Preserve, home base for alligators that fit easily into the whopper category. Don't mess with them but do enjoy a picnic in this lovely spot. The preserve is on Museum Road, a mile west of S.W. Thirteenth Street.

Some fossils that have shed light on Florida's ancient history were found two miles northwest of Gainesville at the **Devil's Millhopper State Geological Site.** This huge five-acre sinkhole has yielded shark teeth and other evidence of the prehistoric sea that once covered the state. Some of the plants and animals in the 120-foot-deep collapsed caverns are more typical of the Appalachian Mountains than of Florida. Off SR 232 (Millhopper Road). Devil's Millhopper State Geological Site, 4732 N.W. Fifty-third Avenue, Gainesville, FL 32601. Open 8:00 A.M. to sunset year-round.

At **O'Leno State Park,** the scenic Sante Fe River performs a real disappearing act as it flows underground for more than three miles before coming to the surface. Other natural features of O'Leno are sinkholes, hardwood hammocks, river swamp and sandhill communities. You'll find a good view of the river from the suspension bridge built by the Civilian Conservation Corps in the late 1930s. A fine place to camp, canoe, fish, swim or walk the nature trails. The park is off U.S. 41, 25 miles northwest of Gainesville. Open 8:00 A.M. to sunset year-round. O'Leno State Park, Rt. 2, Box 1010, High Springs, FL 32643; (904) 454-1853.

Ichetucknee Springs State Park features a pristine crystal-clear river, but it is not exactly undiscovered. Floating down the scenic Ichetucknee in an inner tube has become so popular the park limits tubers to protect vegetation. Spending a day (or a few hours) on this river is a perfectly splendid thing to do. The current moves you effortlessly along so you can enjoy the surrounding beauty. No wonder this is such a popular pastime.

The river's source is a group of springs that boil out of limestone sinks and trickle out from under cypress tree roots to the tune of 233 million gallons a day. Ichetucknee is the state's third largest spring, an impressive statistic in a state that claims more springs than any other.

At the park entrance you will receive a map of tubing options. No food, drink or pets are allowed on the river. The peak season is May through September when the park is apt to be most crowded. At other times, you can occasionally have the river to yourself. The water is 72 degrees year-round. Local vendors rent tubes and canoes. The park, which is north of Gainesville, off I-75, and 4 miles northwest of Fort White, off SR 47 and CR 238, is open 8:00 A.M. to sunset. For maps and details, contact the north entrance of Ichetucknee State Park on CR 238 or call (904) 497–2511.

Off the Beaten Path in Northwest Florida

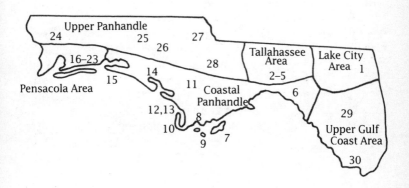

1. Stephen Foster State Folk Culture Center
2. Maclay Ornamental Gardens
3. Lafayette Vineyards and Winery
4. Tallahassee Junior Museum
5. Wakulla Springs
6. St. Marks National Wildlife Refuge
7. St. George Island
8. John Gorrie Museum
9. St. Vincent National Wildlife Refuge
10. St. Joseph Peninsula
11. Dead Lakes State Recreational Area
12. St. Andrews
13. Shell Island
14. Eden State Gardens
15. Temple Mound Museum
16. Gulf Islands National Seashore
17. Fort Pickens
18. Seville Square
19. Pensacola Historical Museum
20. North Hill Preservation District
21. Hopkins' Boarding House
22. Pensacola Naval Aviation Museum
23. Big Lagoon State Recreation Area
24. Blackwater River State Park
25. Lake DeFuniak
26. Falling Waters State Recreation Area
27. Florida Caverns State Park
28. Torreya State Park
29. Forest Capital State Museum
30. Cedar Key

Northwest Florida

Lake City Area

The **Stephen Foster State Folk Culture Center** pays tribute to the man who made the Suwannee River famous, wrote "Old Folks at Home" (Florida's official state song) and gave us such long-standing favorites as "Oh Susannah" and "Camptown Races." One of America's best-loved composers, Stephen Foster was born in Pennsylvania in 1842 and died at the age of thirty-seven in New York City with $.38 in his pocket. He never did get to see the Suwannee, but you should. It's the second largest river in the state, and you may camp, boat, fish and explore nature trails.

The Foster Museum is housed in a antebellum-style mansion that conjures up all sorts of romantic images of the Old South. The Carillon Tower chimes forth hourly concerts of Foster favorites. Inside you may take a trip through yesteryear as you inspect Foster memorabilia, antique musical instruments, original manuscripts and animated dioramas.

The Florida Folk Festival, an annual gathering of folk musicians and craftspeople in May, is a well-attended event. The Jeanie Ball (named for "Jeanie with the Light Brown Hair") is the highlight of October, and December features popular Christmas Concerts. For a complete schedule of events, write Stephen Foster Center, White Springs, FL 32096; (904) 397–2733. The Stephen Foster Center is open every day 9:00 A.M.—5:00 P.M. White Springs is 3 miles east of I-75 and 10 miles northwest of Lake City at the junction of U.S. 41 and SR 136.

For another look at this well-known river, head west for Suwannee River State Park. The overlook above the confluence of the Suwannee and the Withlacoochee provides a commanding view of both rivers as well as a fine place for a picnic. Across the river are the remains of Confederate earthworks built to protect the railroad bridge across the Suwannee. Oaks bearded with moss and cypress trees canopy the tranquil river creating a scenic setting for those who enjoy camping, boating, fishing and hiking. Open 8:00 A.M.—sunset. The park is 13 miles west of Live Oak off U.S. 90; (904) 362–2746.

Tallahassee Area

At the **Maclay Ornamental Gardens** near Tallahassee, the peak blooming season begins in December and continues through April when dogwood, redbud and more than a hundred varieties of camellias and azaleas create a fairyland of flowers. The gardens are an oasis of beauty all year, but spring is spectacular! This 307-acre park was once the home of Alfred B. Maclay, a New York financier who made his winter home here starting in 1923.

He developed the grounds as a hobby, using exotic plants to complement the native varieties and adding reflecting pools and avenues of stately palms. Stroll the brick walkways to the tiny walled garden where a graceful fountain provides the only sound except for the distant coo of the doves. If it's serenity you're after, you've come to the right place. Picnic grounds overlook Lake Hall, which is fine for swimming and boating (only electric motors allowed).

The park is open daily 8:00 A.M. to sundown year-round. The gardens and the Maclay House Museum are open daily 9:00 A.M.—5:00 P.M. January—April. The Maclay Gardens are 5 miles north of Tallahassee on U.S. 319. Alfred B. Maclay State Gardens, 3540 Thomasville Road, Tallahassee, FL 32308; (904) 487–4556 or (904) 487–4115.

The tradition of wintering in Florida was apparently started by Hernando de Soto in 1539. He and his men celebrated Christmas mass in the vicinity of Lake Jackson Mounds State Archaeological Site in what is believed to have been the first Christmas in the New World. That doesn't seem like such a long time ago when you consider that, on the basis of recent excavations, archaeologists now speculate the area was inhabited as early as 1,300 years before Christ.

The dominant features of this state park are impressive pyramid-shaped mounds that are the remains of the largest known Indian ceremonial center in North Florida. A way of life flourished here from A.D. 1300 to 1600 that revolved around a village, six temple mounds and a burial mound. The Indians who lived here were farmers who traded their surplus crops with nearby villages. After you climb to the top of the highest mound, you will more fully appreciate the fact that these mounds were created by Indians carrying sand and clay, one basketful at a time! This is a lovely spot for a picnic and a walk through the woods. The Butler Mill Trail through a hardwood ravine and upland pine woods leads to an early 1880s grist mill site. The mounds are located 6 miles north of Tallahassee off U.S. 27 and are free.

For more information about ancient Florida—its ice age, huge mastodons, resourceful Indians and Spanish explorers—stop in at the Museum of Florida History in downtown Tallahassee. This is the place to learn about Florida's role on the high seas, to inspect a pre–Civil War dugout boat and to view precious gold doubloons. Florida's wild booms and busts, complete with a colorful cast of characters from pirates to lumber tycoons, are all part of the story. Fascinating for all ages, the museum is housed in the R. A. Grey Building (500 S. Bronough) across from the state Supreme Court in Tallahassee. Open every day but Christmas, 9:00 A.M.—4:30 P.M. Monday through Friday 10:00 A.M.—4:30 P.M. Saturday; noon—4:30 P.M. Sundays and holidays, no admission fee; (904) 488–1484.

The LeMoyne Art Center and Sculpture Garden is an oasis of peaceful beauty tucked into the middle of Tallahassee. The area's leading artists are represented in this compact gallery. A few metal sculptures adorn a small but lovingly cared for garden behind the gallery. For information write to LeMoyne Art Foundation, Inc., 125 N. Gadsen Street, Tallahassee, FL 32301. Open Tuesday through Saturday 10:00 A.M.—5:00 P.M., Sunday 1:00—5:00 P.M., closed holidays; (904) 222–8800 or 224–2714. Free.

For a smashing view of this incredibly verdant city, take an elevator ride to the twenty-second—floor observation deck of the Florida State Capitol at Monroe Street and Apalachee Parkway in downtown Tallahassee.

Want the genuine bird's-eye view? Care to drift over lovely old plantations and be surrounded by so much quiet you can hear deer running through the woods? Then sign up for a champagne balloon flight over Tallahassee. No one knows exactly where you'll end up. That depends on the wind. The important thing is to enjoy your experience aloft. A flight for two, which includes a picnic brunch, champagne for the traditional toasts and first flight souvenirs, can be arranged through Aeronauts & Balloons. This shop will take care of all your unusual party and gift needs from balloon bouquets, balloon drops and releases to specially imprinted balloons. Aeronauts & Balloons is located in the shopping center known as The Verandas at 1355 Market Street, Tallahassee, FL 32312; (904) 893–1282.

Still got flying on your mind? The Flying High Circus serves up excitement one weekend every March. Eighty students perform in this three-ring circus at Florida State University at W. Tennessee (U.S. 90) and Copeland streets. Performances are Friday and Saturdays at 8:00 P.M. with a matinee at 2:00 on Saturday afternoon. For details call (904) 644–4874. Campus tours and maps are available at the Visitor Information Center at 100 S. Woodward Street in Tallahassee; (904) 644–3264.

When you think Florida, do visions of orange juice dance in your head? Think again. Would you believe fine wines? A visit to the award-winning **Lafayette Vineyards and Winery** just east of Tallahassee (on land originally given to the Marquis de Lafayette by President James Monroe) should definitely be on tap. French explorers reveled in the area's profusion of wild grapes way back in the mid-sixteenth century. Now it's your turn to sample the nectar of the muscadine and scuppernong grapes.

The folks at Lafayette take their wine tasting seriously and share their knowledge and products enthusiastically with visitors. You'll sip such favorites as Stover, Plantation White, White Muscadine and Red Muscadine. The tasting is free, and you're welcome to buy your favorite. Your wine-loving friends will appreciate a gift from a selection that ranges from fine crystal and books on wines to wine jellies and fancy corkscrews.

This small but modern operation has only been turning out wine since 1983, but vintner Jeanne Burgess reports a warm reception from the local community along with impressive international recognition for some of its wines. After the tasting you'll want to tour the two-story French provincial cellar with its stainless steel tanks, bottling line and walk-in cold room. From an elevated rear deck you'll view a bucolic rural scene of rolling hills and vineyards.

Lafayette Vineyards and Winery is east of Tallahassee at 6505 Mahan Drive, a mile west of exit 31A off I-10. The winery is open year-round 10:00 A.M.—6:00 P.M. Monday through Saturday and noon—6:00 P.M. on Sunday. Tours and tasting are free; call (904) 878–9041.

The **Tallahassee Junior Museum** is a favorite haunt for adults as well as children who are curious about the way things were. At this authentic 1880 pioneer farm and community, you'll see demonstrations of blacksmithing, syrup making, sheep shearing, spinning and weaving. There are nature trails, exhibits of wild animals native to the area, a one-room schoolhouse, grist mill and Bellevue Plantation, once the home of Prince and Princess Murat. The Tallahassee Junior Museum is at 3945 Museum Drive on Lake Bradford bordering Apalachicola National Forest. Open every day 9:00 A.M.—5:00 P.M.; (904) 576–1636.

If you'd like to peer into the world's deepest spring, head south of Tallahassee to **Wakulla Springs** where limestone-filtered water gushes forth at more than 600,000 gallons per minute. Wakulla has been a sanctuary for wildlife and people ever since Indians fished its 185-foot depths and Spanish explorers refreshed themselves in its clean, clear waters. Tourists after the Civil War thought the springs well worth the trip, as did underwater filmmakers, who came as early as the mid-1940s.

The resort still has an old-fashioned flavor due to its emphasis on conservation rather than razzle-dazzle tourism. This 4,000-acre wildlife sanctuary provides a glorious glimpse into precondominium Florida. Jungle cruises and glass-bottom boat tours reveal an enchanting blend of scenery and wildlife. You'll see lots of alligators and elegant birds including snowy egrets, herons and ibis.

One common meaning given for the Indian word **Wakulla** is Mysteries of Strange Waters. The spring has its share of mysteries including complete mastodon skeletons, which have been found in the bottom of the spring. It seems appropriate that this was the location for the filming of *Creature of the Black Lagoon*.

After exploring the nature trails or taking a swim, examine the Indian relics in Wakulla Springs Lodge. This Spanish-style inn, built in the 1930s of Tennessee marble, has unusual wood ceiling beams decorated with Florida scenes and flowers. The lodge dining room serves up Southern cooking at a reasonable cost. (Try the coconut cream pie.) Wakulla Springs is 15 miles south of Tallahassee on Rte. 61. Hours are 9:30 A.M.—5:30 P.M. Wakulla Springs and Lodge, Wakulla Springs, FL 32305; (904) 224–5950.

Civil War buffs will not want to miss the Natural Bridge Battlefield State Historic Site. Young cadets from West Florida Seminary (now Florida State University) and old men (Gadsden County Grays) joined Confederate forces to inflict heavy casualties on Union soldiers here on March 6, 1865. Thanks to their efforts, Tallahassee was the only southern capital east of the Mississippi that did not fall into Union hands. Each year, in early March, the battle is reenacted.

This is a fine place to do a little fishing in the St. Marks River or to have a picnic, but don't go looking for an impressive arch like Virginia's Natural Bridge. This was originally a place where the river flowed underground for a ways, but the county has modified the "bridge" for drainage purposes. The battlefield site is 10 miles southeast of Tallahassee. Take U.S. 363 to Woodville, then go east on Natural Bridge Road (SR 354); (904) 925–6216. Free.

Coastal Panhandle

St. Marks National Wildlife Refuge consists of 90,000 acres of national forests, water areas and the coast on the Gulf of Mexico. Stop in the Headquarters and Visitors Center for a look at the interpretive displays and an observation-deck view of the marsh. Then take the scenic drive to the St. Marks Lighthouse, one of the oldest in the southeast. Constructed in 1831 from stones removed from old Fort San Marcos de Apalache, this lighthouse guides modern vessels with the same lens it used during the Civil War.

This is Florida's only wintering area for Canada geese. If you are a bird-watcher or an alligator watcher, you will be in your glory. (You'll feel even more glorious if you remembered the bug repellent.) Hike the 32 miles of primitive walking trails and enjoy a picnic lunch overlooking the water near the lighthouse. The Visitors Center, 3 miles south of U.S. 98 on Co. Rd. 59, is open 8:00 A.M.—4:30 P.M. Monday through Friday and Saturday and Sunday 10:00 A.M.—5:00 P.M. You are welcome in the refuge anytime during daylight hours to picnic, launch a boat, crab or fish. Call (904) 925–6121.

San Marcos de Apalache State Museum is also the site of a fort first built in 1679 by the Spaniards. The fort was held at various times by the British, Spanish and Confederate forces. Its capture by General Andrew Jackson in 1818 was an important factor in the United States' acquisition of Florida the next year. The museum contains artifacts spanning the area's history from the Spanish occupation to the Civil War. A lovely trail winds through Confederate earthworks, climbs to the top of a powder magazine, follows crumbling fort walls along the banks of the Wakulla River and ends at the original site of early Spanish fortifications where the Wakulla and St. Marks River merge. The museum is 24 miles south of Tallahassee on SR 363 in St. Marks. Open daily 9:00 A.M.—5:00 P.M. San Marcos de Apalache, Box 27, St. Marks, FL 32355; (904) 925–6216.

Right around the corner from the museum is Posey's, "The Home of the Topless Oyster." (Also the home of some terrifically tasty smoked mullet.) The music is jukebox and the decor is strictly split-log picnic tables and beer advertisements. (The calendar is by Coors and the hands of the clock point to Miller Time.) But you did not come for the ambiance or fine china. (Good thing, because the mullet is served on a brown paper towel.) Try a smoked mullet, baked oysters with bacon and cheese or boiled shrimp. The answer to a runaway appetite is a bushel of fresh oysters chased by a cold beer. If you like Posey's famous hot sauce, you may buy a bottle to take home. Posey's, on the road to the museum in St. Marks, is open during the peak oyster season from September to April. Inexpensive.

Folks from Tallahassee head to the coast for fresh seafood, and one of their favorite destinations is Spring Creek Restaurant. This family operation hides out under ive oaks festooned with Spanish moss where, according to

Posey's "Home of the Topless Oyster"

the menu, "fresh spring water merges with the Gulf, creating the finest seafood in the world." Spring Creek serves up generous portions of scamp, mullet, crab fingers, catfish, oysters, lobster, deviled crab and grouper throats, to name just a few. The salad bar comes to the table so you can build your own. Specialties are cheese grits and homemade desserts such as chocolate peanut butter pie and coconut cream pie. You might want to take along a jar of dry mix, which makes eighteen pints of their tasty salad dressing with the addition of your own buttermilk and mayonnaise. Take U.S. 363 (S. Monroe Street) south from Tallahassee, go west on U.S. 98 and south on Co. Rd. 365 to the tiny community of Spring Creek. Open for lunch and dinner. Prices are mostly in the moderate range; (904) 926–3751.

Once you've started, there's no stopping. Fresh seafood is a fun addiction. Angelo's Seafood Restaurant's roomy wrap-around deck is just the place to relax in a rocking chair and have a cocktail while the sun sets over the river. Try the char-broiled mullet, the soft-shell crab or the snapper throats and, for sure, their Greek salad. Each table gets a corked wine bottle full of dressing. Angelo's "over the water" restaurant is right by the bridge in Panacea. Owners Angelo and Arline Petrandis take a lot of pride in their handsome restaurant, which is open Friday and Saturday 4:30— 11:00 P.M., Sunday noon—11:00 P.M., and 4:30—10:00 P.M. every other day but Tuesday. Prices are mostly moderate. Call (904) 984–5168.

You really shouldn't drive through Carrabelle without tipping your hat to the world's smallest police station. You can't miss it. It's a public phone booth right on the main drag with an American flag painted on it. Often the patrol car is parked beside it waiting for the next call. If so, why not wave? Carrabelle doesn't even remotely resemble the Naked City.

Another favorite local spot in Carrabelle is Harry's Bar. You may choose dim interior with cozy booths, TV and pool table or an umbrellaed table in the sunny courtyard. The specialty here is pizza (try it with hot banana peppers), or you might want to check out the rumor that Harry makes the best gyros (pronounced year-o's) north of Tarpon Springs. The Greek salad is a treat as are the spanakopitas (filo turnover filled with spinach, cheeses, eggs, onions, fresh dill and seasonings). If you're into imported beer, you're in the right place. Lunches are inexpensive. Open 11:00 A.M.—midnight every day. Harry's is on Marine Street in Carrabelle; (904) 697–9982.

A British fort once stood at the Fort Gadsden State Historic Site. Held for a time by Indians and runaway slaves, it was destroyed by American forces in 1816. In 1818 Andrew Jackson ordered the fort to be rebuilt, but today only a bare outline is visible. A miniature replica of Fort Gadsden, some British muskets and Indian artifacts are on display in an open-sided interpretive center. You may picnic, go fishing and boating on the Apalachicola River and explore the nature trails. A short walk will take you to the remains of the renegade cemetery where grave robbers left nothing but shallow depressions. Fort Gadsden is 24 miles north of U. S. 98 just off SR 65 (21 miles of good road, the last 3 miles are rough) or 6 miles south of Sumatra off SR 65. Open daily 8:00 A.M.—sunset; (904) 670—8988. Free.

If you love the beach — the sand, the sea and the sky —

uncluttered by honky-tonk attractions, head for **St. George Island** at the end of Apalachicola Bay. The miles of underdeveloped beaches, sand dunes and marshland are not totally wild. You'll find nature trails, boardwalks, observation platforms, picnic and camping areas and bathhouses. This is the place to wade out at low tide and gather oysters, then savor them while you watch the late sun gild the sea oats. Take the turnoff from U.S. 98 that leads across the toll bridge to St. George Island. Open daily 8:00 A.M.—sunset (904) 670–2111.

Apalachicola's Trinity Church, one of the oldest (1830s) in the state, was cut in sections in New York and floated by schooner down the Atlantic Coast and around the Florida Keys. The original church bell was melted down to make Confederate cannon. Trinity, sometimes called the nation's first prefabricated church, is on Sixth Street, a block off U.S. 98, across from the Gorrie Museum in Apalachicola. Free.

Whether you know it or not, you owe a lot to John Gorrie. He's the physician whose inventions make it possible for you to enjoy air conditioning, refrigeration and ice cubes in your drink. Back in the days when ice had to be shipped all the way from the Great Lakes, it was a precious commodity in Florida. Dr. John Gorrie wanted a way to cool the rooms of patients suffering from malaria. The only problem was that the pipes in his experimental machine kept clogging with ice. When he realized the importance of this accidental discovery, he immediately built a small ice-making machine. You may inspect a replica of the machine (patented in 1851) that paved the way for modern refrigeration and air conditioning in the **John Gorrie Museum.** (The original machine is in the Smithsonian Institute.) This one-room museum also has displays on cotton, lumbering, fishing and other aspects of early Apalachicola history. The Museum is at Avenue C and Sixth Street, one block off U.S. 319-98 in Apalachicola. Open 9:00 A.M.—5:00 P.M. daily except Tuesday and Wednesday; (904) 653–9347.

St. Vincent National Wildlife Refuge on St. Vincent Island is a bridgeless gem given over to some rather exotic animals and birds. Whitetail deer, wild hogs, raccoons, opossums and turkey share the triangular-shaped refuge with sambar deer, which were imported from India by early owners. Red-tailed hawks, peregrine falcons, bald eagles and a host of songbirds and waterfowl come and go. The deserted beaches are a favorite nesting ground for sea turtles. Most alligators hang around the freshwater ponds and marshes, while a few individualists choose to sun on the beach and enjoy the surf. Something to remember when taking a swim! This splendid place, with mile after mile of unspoiled beach, can only be reached by water. Contact the refuge manager for information on freshwater fishing, island exploration and managed hunts for deer and wild hog. No charge for using the island, but you'll have to make your own arrangements to get there. Refuge Manager, St. Vincent National Wildlife Refuge, P.O. Box 447, Apalachicola, FL 32320; (904) 653–8808.

St. Joseph Peninsula (T. H. Stone Memorial) is a lovely stretch of sand bordered on one side by St. Josephs Bay and on the other by the Gulf of Mexico. Majestic sand dunes tower to heights of 60 feet. Saltwater marshes attract large bird populations, especially in the fall when between 3,000 and 5,000 migrating hawks stop in the park. This is the only area in Northwest Florida where the endangered peregrine falcon may be seen with regularity. Campsites and family cottages are available. The peninsula is across the bay from Port St. Joe on SR 30E; (904) 227–1327.

If you would like to see where the first of Florida's five constitutions was written, stop in at the Constitution Convention State Museum. Here you'll view an impressive replica of the Convention Hall's west wing, see eighteenth-century artifacts and learn the story of the town of St. Joseph, which vanished forever after the 1844 hurricane. Outside exhibits include an antique railroad and a plaque commemorating Florida's first railroad. The museum is a quarter mile east of U.S. 98, just south of Port St. Joe. Open Thursday through Monday 9:00 A.M.—5:00 P.M.; (904) 229–8029.

Strange as it may seem, the Dead Lakes are alive with fish. Named for thousands of cypress, oak and pine trees that drowned in the natural overflow of the Chipola River, **Dead Lakes State Recreation Area** enjoys a reputation as one of the best freshwater fishing spots in the Florida Panhandle. A longleaf pine forest shelters a tranquil picnic and camping area, and large stands of bare trees create a place of haunting beauty. One mile north of Wewahitchka on SR 71. Dead Lakes State Recreation Area, P.O. Box 989, Wewahitchka, FL

32465; (904) 639-2702. No charge for day use.

Another state recreation area that takes advantage of the Panhandle's gloriously white beaches is **St. Andrews** near Panama City. The water is unusually clear, the dunes are picturesque, and the pine woods shade fine campsites. Be sure to take a look at the restored old-time "cracker" turpentine still. St. Andrews is 3 miles east of Panama City Beach on SR 392, 4415 Thomas Drive, Panama City, FL 32408. Open 8:00 A.M.—sunset; (904) 234–2522.

One of the most popular boat trips along the Panhandle Gulf Coast is to **Shell Island.** This undeveloped treasure of long, white beaches and windswept dunes is perfect for barefoot beachcombers and those who enjoy long, uninterrupted views of the Gulf between swims. Seven and a half miles long and more than a mile wide, this pristine island boasts a freshwater lake and teems with wildlife. From St. Andrews State Park, boats leave four times daily for the western end of the island. Shell Island trips leave for the eastern end of the island from Captain Anderson's Marina on Thomas Drive at Grand Lagoon in Panama City. Boats make the trip twice daily from mid-May to mid-September at 9:00 A.M. and 1:00 P.M. Inquire about sightseeing and dinner cruises. Call (904) 234–3435. From Treasure Island Marina at Grand Lagoon on Panama City Beach, the *Island Star* departs twice daily for a forty-minute ride to the middle of Shell Island where the Hurricane Island Beach Club serves everything from burgers to steak suppers. (An aggressive hurricane ripped Shell Island from the mainland, which was the reason for its first name—Hurricane Island.)

Farther up the coast, the landscaped grounds and mansion of **Eden State Gardens** overlook Choctawhatchee Bay. Once the hub of a large sawmill complex, the lumber baron's antebellum residence now stands alone framed by gnarled oaks dripping with Spanish moss. The stately white columned mansion with a fireplace in every room preserves a fragment of the 1800s, the Old South that has mostly gone with the wind. You may picnic, fish and take a guided tour of this splendid house. Five miles north of Grayton Beach, Eden State Gardens is 1 mile off U.S. 98 at Point Washington. Tours of the house are offered Thursday through Monday on the hour, 9:00 A.M.—4:00 P.M., and the park is open daily 8:00

A.M.—sunset. Eden State Gardens, P.O. Box 26, Point Washington, FL 32454; (904) 231–4214.

Few places are prettier than Grayton Beach State Recreation Area with its blue-green waters and white-white sand dunes crested by dense stands of sea oats. Artists come here to capture the beauty of trees stunted and sculpted by wind and salt spray. Swimming and camping are popular, of course, and this is a fine place to fish—either in the surf or in the brackish waters of Western Lake. About 25 miles east of Fort Walton Beach by way of U.S. 98 and SR 30A. Grayton State Recreation Area, Rt. 2, Box 790-1, Santa Rosa Beach, FL 32459; (904) 231–4210.

Rocky Bayou State Recreation Area provides an opportunity to see what the real Florida looks like. Located within Eglin Air Force Base, this park sits on the arm of Choctawhatchee Bay known as Rocky Bayou. A freshwater lake by the unlikely name of Puddin Head is home to largemouth bass, alligators and a colony of beavers, and nature trails wind through a sand forest shading reindeer moss and scrub oaks. The area is good for camping, swimming, boating and fishing. Three miles east of Niceville off SR 20. Fred Gannon Rocky Bayou State Recreation Area, Rte. 1, Box 597, Niceville, FL 32578; (904) 897–3222.

How do you like your mullet—smoked, baked, broiled, fried or in gumbo? The great thing about the Boggy Bayou Mullet Festival is that you don't have to decide—you can try it every which way. In the early 1900s, mullet was a very important food source as well as the primary livelihood for most of the settlers that lived in this area. Mullet were caught, salted and shipped by boat first to Pensacola, then to other communities in the South.

Of course, the festival offers plenty of other tempting things to eat including specialties from many foreign lands, and you can feast your eyes on the Queen of the Mullet Festival Pageant. Between the canoe races and sailing regattas, tennis and skeet tournaments and the street dance, there is ample action during this three-day extravaganza. The Boggy Bayou Mullet Festival is held the third weekend in October at College Boulevard and Highway 85 north of Niceville. The festival address is P.O. Box 231, Niceville, FL 32578. Admission, parking and nonstop professional entertainment are all free.

Local history takes on new meaning at the Historical Society Museum in Valparaiso. Besides an extensive library of old documents and maps (including *The Complete and Official Records of the Union and Confederate Armies*), the museum houses a collection of artifacts that provides insight into the challenges faced by prehistoric Indians and early pioneers. You'll want to inspect the steam-powered cotton gin as well as tools used in farming, lumbering and producing turpentine. Classes are offered in weaving, quilt-making, needlepoint, tatting and basket-weaving, and handcrafted items are for sale. The Historical Society Museum is at 115 Westview Avenue in downtown Valparaiso. Open Tuesday through Saturday 10:00 A.M.—4:00 P.M.; (904) 678-2615. Free.

At Eglin Air Force Base, you may tour a climatic laboratory, which can reproduce any weather condition from Arctic blizzard to tropical monsoon. For those who like impressive statistics, this laboratory is the largest of its kind in the free world, and Eglin, at 728 square miles, is the largest air force base in the entire world. If you want to see the snow fly, browse the Air Force Armament Museum or catch a military dog demonstration. Free tour tickets are available at the chambers of commerce of Fort Walton, Destin and Twin City. Eglin Air Force Base is 13 miles northeast of Fort Walton Beach. Tour schedules change rather frequently so your best bet is to call for information at (904) 244–8191 or 882–3933. Free.

The historic fishing village of Destin was founded in the 1830s when Captain Leonard A. Destin sailed into Choctawhatchee Bay and decided it was a fine place to raise his family. The two-room Old Destin Post Office Museum is full of artifacts and photos that tell of the early days of this community. If you want to know more about life in "Old Destin," a short history of the village titled ". . . And the Roots Run Deep" is for sale. (Proceeds go to support the museum.) The staff may be able to help with genealogical research on early Destin families. The museum is on Stahlman Avenue, across from the Destin Library and behind Hardee's in Destin. Open Monday and Wednesday 1:30—4:30 P.M. Old Destin Post Office Museum, P.O. Box 691, Destin, FL 32541–0691. No admission fee and no charge for guided tour. (904) 837–8572.

In 1933 the isolated fishing village of Destin underwent a

dramatic change. A wooden bridge was built connecting it to the outside world. Before long, folks began to notice Destin was not only the "luckiest fishing village," but also had some of the finest beaches anywhere. The pilings of that old bridge now add to the nautical atmosphere in Scampi's Seafood and Spirits Restaurant. Who can resist the steam bucket for two consisting of stone crab claws, shrimp, Apalachicola oysters, snowcrab and Louisiana crawfish, corn on the cob, garden salad and French bread. The chef does creative things with fresh vegetables and makes a tasty Key lime pie from an original "conch" recipe. Scampi's is across from The Back Porch on U.S. 98 in East Destin. Open 4:30—10:30 P.M. everyday. Moderate to expensive.

Indians were dining on fresh seafood long before the Europeans "discovered" Florida. Some of them were mound builders, and they left a fine example of their work on the main drag in Fort Walton Beach. Imagine 500,000 basketloads of dirt hauled one at a time to create this impressive landmark.

To learn more about the seven pre-Columbian cultures who inhabited this area over a span of over 10,000 years, drop in at the Indian **Temple Mound Museum** on the east flank of the mound. Here you'll see the re-creation of an ancient temple, a four-legged bowl that has been called the most unique ceramic artifact in the Southeast and various artifacts from recent archaeological excavations.

The museum and mound (which is a National Historic Landmark), at 139 Miracle Strip Parkway on U.S. 98, are owned and operated by the City of Fort Walton Beach. The mound may be viewed during daylight hours and is free. The museum is open Tuesday through Saturday 11:00 A.M.—4:00 P.M. (904) 243-6521.

Remember the school bell, potbelly stove, ink wells, lunch pails, bonnets and straw hats? Then you will want to take a short trip down memory lane to the Camp Walton School House Museum. Painted a gleaming white and refurbished to appear as it did during its prime from 1912 to 1936, the schoolhouse is at 107 First Street in Fort Walton Beach. Open Tuesday and Thursday 9 A.M.—4 P.M. and Wednesday 9 A.M.—2 P.M. Free.

Once upon a time a buccaneer known as Billy Bowlegs

decided being a run-of-the-mill pirate wasn't classy enough. So he assembled a group of followers—Indians, deserters, bandits and the like—and proclaimed himself King of Florida. He did all the things pirates were supposed to do—scared folks out of their wits, took their money and buried it and, in general, made a nuisance of himself. For more than thirty years Fort Walton Beach has been annually reviving his swashbuckling spirit in the rollicking Billy Bowlegs Festival. The first week in June erupts in mock pirate attacks, parades, concerts, ski shows, boat races, crafts exhibits and, of course, treasure hunts. For information write Greater Fort Walton Beach Chamber of Commerce, 34 Miracle Strip Parkway S.E., Fort Walton Beach, FL 32548; (904) 244–8191.

Pensacola Area

Beach lovers can rest easy. **Gulf Islands National Seashore** protects shimmering white sand and swaying sea oats along a 150-mile stretch of islands and keys between Destin, Florida, and Gulfport, Mississippi. The Florida section of the national seashore includes Naval Live Oaks Reservation (where you may hike through groves once prized for ship building), part of Perdido Key, the forts on the Pensacola Naval Air Station and part of Santa Rosa Island.

At the western end of Santa Rosa are the ruins of **Fort Pickens,** which saw action during the Civil War and where Apache chief Geronimo was held prisoner for two ignominious years. Today the beach gets better use as a bird sanctuary and camping and recreation site. Ask the park rangers to recommend the best scuba diving locations. Besides the usual beach activities, you'll want to explore the remains of this massive five-sided fort and visit the small museum. Take U.S. 98 and SR 399 south to Pensacola Beach, then follow signs west to Fort Pickens. Museum opens daily 9:00 A.M.—5:00 P.M. For information: Superintendent, Gulf Islands National Seashore, P. O. Box 100, Gulf Breeze, FL 32561; (904) 932–5302.

Fisherfolk should not miss the opportunity to drop a line from the "world's longest fishing pier," as the old Pensacola Bay Bridge is now known. Judging from the number of fishing poles sprouting from the bridge, this is one hot spot. And no through traffic interferes with your concentration. Easy to find, this bridge parallels the new Pensacola Bay Bridge.

The heart of Pensacola is in **Seville Square,** a historic district between E. Government and S. Alcaniz streets where shops, restaurants, museums and art galleries inhabit a hodgepodge of restored eighteenth- and nineteenth-century cottages and mansions. Pick up a free map and brochures at the Visitor Information Center, 1401 E. Gregory Street (at the foot of the bridge), Pensacola, FL 32501; (904) 434–1234.

Stop in at the **Pensacola Historical Museum** in Old Christ Church, the oldest church building still standing in the state. Once used by the Union Army as a barracks and hospital, the church now is a repository of local history including everything from displays on ancient Indian culture and Mardi Gras costumes to a fully equipped 1915 kitchen. 405 S. Adams Street at Zaragoza Street, Pensacola, FL; (904) 433–1559. Open Monday to Saturday 9:00 A.M.—4:30 P.M. Free.

The West Florida Museum of History, housed in a converted warehouse, features exhibits on the Seminole Indians, Spanish breast plates and helmets from the sixteenth century, great wooden chests and a magnificent hand-carved bed among other treasures. 200 E. Zaragoza Street in Pensacola. Open Monday through Saturday 10:00 A.M.—4:30 P.M., closed Sunday. (904) 434–1042. Free.

Take the kids to the Transportation Museum to see the restored trolley and collection of buggies and be sure to look around in the interesting little shops. The museum is in a restored fish warehouse at 203 E. Zaragoza Street in Pensacola and is open Monday through Saturday during regular business hours. Free.

Not to be missed is Seville Quarter with Rosie O'Grady's Good Time Emporium and seven other saloons and restaurants. Even if you're not hungry, thirsty or in need of entertainment, you really should stop in for a look. Besides an impressive collection of local antiques, the gaslights are from Liverpool, the parliament benches are from London, the disco booth was once an English pulpit, the ships' wheels in Coppersmith's Gallery are from schooners that made tea and spice runs to China, and Rosie's main door at one time graced a mansion in Mobile.

Seville Quarter overflows with choices. Should you down a Flaming Hurricane drink at Rosie's, catch the show on big screen TV in Lili Marlene's World War I Aviators Pub or tap your feet to Apple Annie's wonderful bluegrass music? While you're deciding you might want to order red beans and rice, jambalaya or beignet doughnuts in the Palace Oyster Bar. For an inexpensive lunch, choose oysters on the half shell or a cajun sausage sandwich. Those great pub mirrors on the walls were imported from Edinburgh, Scotland. The Seville Quarter is at 130 E. Government Street in Pensacola, and the prices range from inexpensive to expensive. (904) 434–6211.

Take a ride, or better yet a walk, through **North Hill Preservation District.** This 50-block area, bounded by LaRua, Palafox, Blount and Reus streets, is a treasure trove of fancy turn-of-the-century houses. You'll be able to appreciate the details—the wide verandas, turrets and elaborate ginger-bread trim—better on foot. Maps and touring information are free from the Visitor Information Center (open 9:00 A.M.—5:00 P.M.), 1401 E. Gregory Street, at the foot of Pensacola Bay Bridge.

All your roaming through the North Hill Preservation District is sure to give you a stupendous appetite. You'll need it if you try to do justice to the good southern cooking at **Hopkins' Boarding House.** This bustling establishment is the real thing, an authentic boarding house where you join other diners at big round tables and get to try out your boarding house reach. The place is usually pretty packed, and you may have to wait a few moments to be seated. If so, just grab a rocking chair on the wraparound porch and think ravenous thoughts.

Most first-timers are overwhelmed by the great steaming bowls of food that are replaced before they are emptied. A recent offering included fried chicken, rice, gravy, cole slaw, potato salad, corn muffins, black-eyed peas, cucumber salad, greens, succotash, macaroni and cheese, cake, jello and lots of ice tea. Before you get so stuffed you can hardly see, take a look around at the religious pictures, collections of plates and family photographs that adorn the walls.

You are expected to clear your own plate and to pay cash. Hopkins' Boarding House is at 900 N. Spring Street in the North Hill Preservation District of Pensacola; (904) 438–3979.

Opens at 11:00 A.M. Tuesday through Saturday for lunch and 5:15—7:00 P.M. for dinner. Inexpensive.

The expansive **Pensacola Naval Aviation Museum** is a real prize—a beautifully designed, fascinating tribute to aviation history on the grounds of the world's largest naval air station. You'll follow the growth and development of our country's naval aviation from the first aircraft the Navy purchased in 1911 (replica) to the Skylab command module. Especially fascinating is the movie of the inspiring *Great Flight,* the first successful crossing of the Atlantic Ocean by air in 1919. The only museum in the world devoted exclusively to naval aviation, this one has something for everyone. You can try out the controls of a jet trainer, wander among forty full-size aircraft or browse the book store and gift shop. Use the main entrance of the Naval Air Station. In Pensacola take Palafox Street south to Garden Street, which becomes Navy Boulevard (SR 295). Follow the signs to the Naval Air Station; (904) 452–3604. Open 9:00 A.M.—5:00 P.M. A real bargain, it's free.

The Naval Air Station features a number of other attractions visitors sometimes miss because they simply don't realize they are so close by. The Spanish Fort San Carlos de Barrancas (part of the Gulf Islands National Seashore) is practically across the road from the museum. First, stop in the visitor center to get some background information, then explore the fort and enjoy its commanding view. Be careful in the dark, steep and sometimes slippery tunnel to the water battery.

You can't enter the Old Pensacola Lighthouse, but as you drive by it's nice to know it has been operating since 1825. You will also want to take a look at Sherman Field, home of the famous precision flying team known as the Blue Angels. The Pensacola Naval Air Station main entrance is on Navy Boulevard, SR 295. Free.

While you're in the area, take advantage of the fine facilities at **Big Lagoon State Recreation Area** where you may picnic, camp, boat, fish and swim. An elaborate boardwalk network and observation tower at East Beach provide bird-watchers with an excellent view overlooking the marsh. This is definitely the place to watch the great blue heron stalking his dinner! Also, you may soak up panoramic vistas of Big Lagoon, the park and Gulf Islands National Seashore across the Intracoastal Waterway. The park is about 10 miles southwest of Pensacola off SR 292. Big Lagoon State Recreation Area, 12301 Gulf Beach Highway, Pensacola, FL 32507; (904) 492–1595.

Upper Panhandle

Canoeists and campers will appreciate **Blackwater River State Park** on the shores of one of the cleanest rivers in the country. Below graceful strands of Spanish moss, dark water contrasts with dazzling white sandbars at the riverbends. Especially good for novice paddlers, the river winds its way from Alabama to Blackwater Bay at the leisurely rate of 3 to 4 mph. The park is 15 miles northeast of Milton, 3 miles off U.S. 90. Blackwater River State Park, Rte. 1, Box 57-C, Holt, FL 32564; (904) 623–2363.

Put on your hiking shoes and heed the call of the Jackson Red Ground Hiking Trail. Located in Blackwater River State Forest, this old 21-mile Indian trading trail was used by Gen. Andrew Jackson on his historic 1818 journey to the Florida Territory. Follow the red paint marks on trees from Karick Lake to the Red Rock Picnic Area over a combination of footpaths and forest roadways.

The Jackson Trail, which is part of the National Recreation Trail System and designated as a section of the Florida Trail System, has two camping shelters with hand water pumps along the way. For information weekdays 7:00 A.M.—4:00 P.M., contact Blackwater Forestry Center, Rte. 1, Box 77, Milton, FL 32570; (904) 957–4201. At other times, park rangers are available at the Krul Recreation Area and the Coldwater Recreation Area.

What if you are overcome by a craving for pizza and you happen to be in Crestview, Florida? Consider yourself lucky and head on down to the Hideaway on Main Street. The dough is made from scratch twice daily, the sausage is cut, ground and seasoned on the premises, and the sauce, according to a special recipe, is made fresh every morning. The Hideaway takes pride in not using any artificial emulsifiers or preservatives; its salad bar is crispy fresh, and a glass partition gives you a view of its immaculate kitchen.

The Hideaway is at 210 S. Main Street in Crestview. Open Tuesday through Thursday 11:00 A.M.—9:00 P.M., Friday and Saturday 11:00 A.M.—10:00 P.M., closed Sunday and Monday. To order ahead or place a takeout order: (904) 682–3225. Inexpensive.

Lake DeFuniak, halfway between Pensacola and Tallahassee, is well worth a visit. For one thing, this claims to be one of two perfectly round lakes in the world, and, for another, the area has a rich and fascinating heritage. During the 1880s a railroad executive envisioned a splendid winter resort here. Later, the Chautauqua Committee decided this would make a fine winter site for its program of concerts and lectures given each summer at Lake Chautauqua, New York. Take some time to admire the late nineteenth-century Chautauqua Assembly Building and the grand, old homes that surround the lake. The Great Depression ended this glorious era, but an annual festival helps preserve memories of the past. The lake is in DeFuniak Springs near U.S. 90 and SR 83. For information on the festival held each year in May, call the Walton County Chamber of Commerce; (904) 892-3191.

Don't miss seeing one of the town's most historically significant structures, the Walton-DeFuniak Public Library. Opened on December 20, 1887, this is believed to be the state's oldest public library continuously operating in its original building. Its one room measured 24 by 17 feet and cost just under $580. This charming library holds 20,000 volumes, including some rare books as old as the library itself.

You really wouldn't expect to find a fine European armor collection in such a modest little library, but that is one of the bonuses of getting off the beaten path. When Wallace Bruce was ambassador to Scotland living in Edinburgh in the 1880s, his son Kenneth began collecting armor. The family came to DeFuniak Springs about 1890 when Mr. Bruce became president of the Chautauqua winter program. Some of the pieces of this unusual collection date back as far as the Crusades (1100—1300). Besides European pieces, there are Kentucky rifles from the Daniel Boone era.

The entire collection was willed to Palmer College, but when the college closed in the 1930s, it was given to the city in partial payment of its debts. The city had no suit-

Walton-DeFuniak Public Library

able place for it, so it eventually wound up in the library for you to enjoy. You won't have any trouble finding the library. Just drive around Lake DeFuniak and look for a tiny building. The library's phone number is (904) 892–3624.

Waterfalls in Florida? Strange as it may seem, they do exist in **Falling Waters State Recreation Area.** While they don't exactly create a neck-craning Niagara, these waters do, just the same, fall. You see, some of the most notable geological features in Florida are its sinkholes. A small stream meanders into a 100-foot sink hole, and, viola, a "waterfall!" A few caveats—you will be looking down, not up, and during the dry season there may not be any water to fall.

Not to worry. This forested area, the site of the first attempt (1919) to find oil in Florida, is lovely to stroll through. Limestone sinks, honeycombing the hilly terrain, may be viewed from a series of boardwalks. Take the self-guiding nature trails, picnic, camp and swim. Located 3 miles south of Chipley, off SR 77A, the area is open 8:00 A.M.—sunset year-round. Falling Water State Recreation Area, Rte. 5, Box 660, Chipley, FL 32428; (904) 638–4030.

Florida's caverns are another feature to come under the heading of strange quirks of geology. Over the millennium, mineral-rich drops of water have created the enchanting formations in **Florida Caverns State Park.** Among other sights, you'll see the Waterfall Room, the Cathedral Room and the Wedding Room—all decked out in natural splendor. The caverns are as impressive, if not as large, as some of the country's most famous underground attractions. An enlightening audio-visual show in the visitor center explains how the caverns were formed, and exhibits on natural and cultural history shed some light on the early Indians who found shelter here.

The park also has a disappearing river, a natural bridge and a white sand beach rimming Blue Hole Springs. You may camp, swim, fish, canoe and picnic. The park, off SR 167, is 3 miles north of Marianna. Open 8:00 A.M.—sunset. Florida Caverns State Park, Marianna, FL 32446; (904) 482–9598.

If New England and Canada seem a trifle far to go for fall color, try **Torreya State Park.** Here rugged bluffs and ravines forested by flowers and hardwoods common to the North Georgia Appalachians provide the state's prettiest autumn display. The park, known as a botanist's paradise, protects the Torreya tree, which is native only to the 20-mile surrounding area. Be sure to tour the restored Gregory mansion (1849), once home of an affluent cotton planter, and hike the trails to the Apalachicola River. The park, on SR 271 (which is off SR 12) between Bristol and Greensboro, is open 8:00 A.M.—sunset year-round. Guided tours of the house are given during the week at 10.00 A.M. and on weekends and holidays at 10.00 A.M., 2:00 P.M., and 4:00 P.M.; Torreya State Park, Rte. 2, Box 70, Bristol, FL 32321; (904) 643–2674.

The fishing is fine at Three Rivers State Recreation Area. Named for the Chattahoochee and Flint rivers, which merge to form the Apalachicola, this scenic area includes 4 miles of shoreline on Lake Seminole at the Florida–Georgia border. Home to a slew of alligators and huge alligator snapping turtles as well as fish, Three Rivers is the place to wet a line, boat, picnic or camp. A mile north of Sneads off SR 271. Open 8:00 A.M.—sunset year-round. Three Rivers State Recreation Area, Rte. 1, Box 15-A, Sneads, FL 32460; (904) 482–9006.

Upper Gulf Coast

The **Forest Capital State Museum,** just south of Perry ("Tree Capital of the South"), pays tribute to forestry, the state's third largest industry. This cypress geodesic dome features an old turpentine still, as well as exhibits on such things as modern day turpentine production and the sex life of the pine tree. After learning about Florida's 314 known species of trees and the 5,000 products manufactured from the longleaf pine tree, take time to wander through the turn-of-the-century Cracker Homestead behind the visitor center.

This log cabin home has a "dog trot" (a breezeway), mosquito netting on the beds and a kitchen that is separated from the house in case of fire. Near the well, tubs for washing clothes stand ready for action. (Keep in mind, these are the "good, old days.") A grape arbor, outhouse, pantry house, chicken pen, barn, corn crib, cane grinder and smokehouse round out the self-sufficient scene of yesteryear.

The Visitor Center Museum and Cracker Homestead are off U.S. 98-27A just south of Perry. The center is open 9:00 A.M.—5:00 P.M. every day except Tuesday and Wednesday, Thanksgiving, Christmas and New Year's days. Forest Capital State Museum, 204 Forest Park Drive, Perry, FL 32347; (904) 584–3227. In October the Florida Forest Festival celebrates by crowning a Forestry Queen and holding chainsaw championships, arts and crafts shows and the world's largest fish fry.

If you're in the area and the sun is beginning to set, take SR 51 toward Steinhatchee. This is the precondo Florida that those who love to hunt and fish cherish. This is also a perfect setting for Cooey's Restaurant, started in the lean days of the Depression and enlarged, by popular demand, over the years. Elizabeth Cooey remembers the excitement of fall fishing, when the trout and redfish made an annual run up the river, and she recalls how their lives changed after electricity came to town in 1945. Try the Seafood Sample of mullet, shrimp, scallops, oysters, deviled crab, blue crab-claws and catfish. Most entrees fall into the moderate category. You might want to buy a pint of palmetto guava jelly or Cooey's fish chowder to enjoy at home. Cooey's is on the main road in Steinhatchee. (904) 498–3501. Moderate.

Halfway between Tallahassee and Tampa but a world apart from both, **Cedar Key** is far enough off the beaten interstate to have preserved the flavor of old Florida. (Take SR 24 off I-19 and 98.) This tiny fishing village is on the largest of more than a hundred islands clustered in the Gulf of Mexico. Three miles from the mainland, Cedar Key is officially on Way Key, which is connected to the mainland by causeway. Local restaurants, the beneficiaries of fishing, crabbing, scalloping and oystering, are known for their sumptuous repasts.

Settled in the early 1840s, Cedar Key began to blossom in 1861 with the completion of Florida's first major railroad, which ran from Fernandina in the northeast corner of the state to Cedar Key. This led to a boom in the lumber business and brought trainloads of tourists. It seems incredible today, but Cedar Key was once the second largest city in Florida.

After the Civil War, Cedar Key developed a reputation as a center for shipbuilding and manufacturing wooden pencils. When the cedar forests had all been leveled, residents turned to the sea for their living. For a brief time the manufacture of brushes and brooms from palmetto fiber created a flurry of business activity, but the discovery of plastics decisively ended that enterprise. As if it needed a final "blow," this once-bustling port was devastated by the hurricane of 1896, from which it never fully recovered.

All these ups and downs are carefully documented at two pleasant little museums, Cedar Key State Museum and the Cedar Key Historical Society Museum. The State Museum, on Museum Drive, is open 9:00 A.M.—5:00 P.M.; (904) 543–5350. The Cedar Key Historical Society Museum, on the corner of Second and D streets, is open Monday through Friday 10:00 A.M.—5:00 P.M. and Sunday 1:00—5:00 P.M.

Cedar Key's National Wildlife Refuge, covering three islands, gives rattlesnakes the same preferential treatment as birds. Sea views are embellished by the pink flash of a rare roseate spoonbill, freewheeling frigates and pelicans crashing into the Gulf in search of supper. The refuge is strictly an environmental study area and not open for visitor use. But bird-watchers who rent a boat and cruise near the islands will be well rewarded.

Festival followers flock to the Cedar Key Sidewalk Arts Festival in April and the Seafood Festival in mid-October. For information, contact the Cedar Key Area Chamber of Commerce at Second Street and SR 24 or call (904) 543–5600.

Off the Beaten Path in Central Florida

Ocala Area
18–20

Eastern Interior

6   1,2

21

5

Orlando Area

Central Atlantic Coast

3,4

22

Gulf Coast   7–14

23

15

16

25,26   27

28   29   24

30

Central Heartland

17

Tampa—St. Petersburg Area

1. Daytona International Speedway
2. Museum of Arts and Sciences
3. Canaveral National Seashore
4. Merritt Island Wildlife Preserve
5. Blue Springs State Park
6. Hontoon Island State Park
7. Scenic Boat Tour
8. U.S. Navy Recruit Graduation Exercises
9. Loch Haven Park
10. Walt Disney World's Fort Wilderness Campground
11. Church Street Station
12. Gatorland Zoo
13. Medieval Times Dinner Tournament
14. Kissimmee Chain-of-Lakes
15. Bok Tower Gardens
16. Lake Kissimmee State Park and 1876 Cow Camp
17. Highlands Hammock State Park
18. Thoroughbred farms
19. Ocala National Forest
20. Silver Springs
21. Homosassa Springs Wildlife Park
22. Weeki Wachee Springs
23. Tarpon Springs
24. Ybor City and Ybor Square
25. Honeymoon Island State Recreation Area
26. Caladesi Island
27. Kapok Tree Restaurant
28. Suncoast Seabird Sanctuary
29. Salvador Dali Museum
30. Fort DeSoto Park

Central Florida

Central Atlantic Coast

Ormond Beach and Daytona Beach owe their starts to the irrepressible Henry Flagler, who extended his railroad south and built the ornate Hotel Ormond in the late 1880s. The monied set was not far behind. When the Vanderbilts, Astors and Goulds started wintering in Ormond Beach, it became known as the "millionaire's colony."

Rich men shipped their automobiles to Florida because the 500-foot-wide beach with its hard-packed sand was perfect for running flat out. By the turn of the century, Henry Ford, Louis Chevrolet and R. E. Olds were comparing times on the beach's measured mile. Things moved quickly. In 1903 Alexander Winton set a world record of 68 mph on the sands of Daytona. A Stanley Steamer was clocked at 127.66 mph in 1906. The next year Ralph Owens made the first car trip from New York to Daytona in an amazing seventeen days. Thirteen auto speed records were set here between 1902 and 1935, earning the area the reputation as the "birthplace of speed."

Faster cars and larger crowds gradually outgrew the oval raceway that had been dug into the Daytona dunes. A 2 1/2-mile asphalt track, opened in 1959, offered new challenges to the growing sport. World attention is riveted on the famous **Daytona International Speedway** during the July 4th 400-mile stock car race and its Daytona 500 in February. No tours of the Speedway are offered during races and special tests, but at other times a one-half-hour bus tour will fill you in on all the details. Open 9:00 A.M.—5:00 P.M. daily. The Speedway is at 1801 Speedway Boulevard. For tickets to special events, write Daytona International Speedway, P.O. Drawer S, Daytona, FL 32015; (904) 253–6711.

Daytona Beach's **Museum of Arts and Sciences** has a fine collection of Cuban paintings, a skeleton of a giant ground sloth, interesting fossils and a planetarium with musical laser light shows. Open daily, except Monday, 9:00 A.M.—4:00 P.M. At 1040 Museum Boulevard in Tuscawilla Park; (904) 255–0285.

The area around New Smyrna Beach was anticipating a sweet future until rampaging Indians burned its sugar mill in 1835 during the Second Seminole War. Today coquina-block foundation and walls, some machinery and restored kettles are all that remain of the old (1763) mill. Located off SR 44 on Mission Drive. New Smyrna Sugar Mill Ruins State Historic Site, P.O. Box 861, New Smyrna Beach, FL 32170. Open daily, (904) 428–2126. Free.

Holiday mail, as you might imagine, is big business in the Christmas Post Office. Each December, thousands of out-of-towners bring their cards or mail them so they will be remailed and carry a Christmas postmark. (Some mail arrives from as far away as Europe and the Orient.) The former postmaster of Christmas, Juanita Tucker, lives next door to the post office and gives tours by appointment only. Ask in the post office.

The Kennedy Space Center, just south of Titusville, is flanked by the **Canaveral National Seashore** and the sprawling Merritt Island National Wildlife Refuge. All that's left of 600 years of fresh oyster dinners consumed by early Florida Indians is the 40-foot historic Turtle Mound at the northern tip of the National Seashore. Because this shell mound was the highest point of land for miles around, it served as an important landmark and appeared on sixteenth-century maps. Climb the boardwalk to the top for an impressive view of river and ocean. Turtle Mound is 10 miles south of New Smyrna Beach on SR A1A. Canaveral National Seashore is 7 miles east of Titusville. Open during daylight hours, the Turtle Mound is free.

Swimmers, surfers and beachcombers head for Playalinda Beach at the south end of Canaveral where sea oats and shifting dunes create a lovely seascape. The National Seashore is one of the last sections of undeveloped beach on the east coast of Florida. The beach, open during daylight hours (except when the road is closed due to NASA launch-related activities), is free.

The **Merritt Island Wildlife Preserve** protects more endangered species of birds, mammals and reptiles than any other area of the continental United States. The Audubon Society has registered one of the highest counts of bird species in the country here. Gulls, terns, egrets, herons, ibis and storks are a common sight. You may even be lucky enough to spot the pretty pink roseate spoonbill or the endangered bald eagle. Open during daylight hours; (305) 867–4820. Free.

If you are intrigued by tropical foliage, you will want to take the Dent Smith Trail on the grounds of the Florida Institute of Technology in Melbourne and see more than 300 species of palms, ferns and other plants. The institute is on Country Club Road, a mile south of New Haven Avenue, Melbourne; (904) 781–4000.

Eastern Interior

The endangered manatees have long made **Blue Springs State Park** their winter home. These large mammals congregate in Blue Springs Run between November and March because the year-round 72-degree water offers a refuge from the chilly St. Johns River. You may view these large "sea cows" (adults weigh about a ton) from observation platforms along Blue Spring Run. Once common from the Carolinas to Texas, these gentle giants now survive only in Florida, and this is one of the few places you may observe them in their native habitat. A two-hour boat ride explores the St. Johns River and the area around Hontoon Island.

In 1872 the Thursby family built a big frame house on the top of an ancient snail shell mound. The house and grounds have been restored to look as they did in the 1880s when oranges grew in the yard and the family sent their crops to Jacksonville by steamboat. The park is a fine place to camp (six family vacation cabins available), canoe, swim, fish, picnic, snorkel and scuba dive. Located 2 miles west of Orange City off I-4 and U.S. 17, the park opens at 8:00 A.M. and closes at sunset year-round. Blue Spring State Park, 2100 W. French Avenue, Orange City, FL 32763; (904) 775–3663.

The only way to reach **Hontoon Island State Park** is by boat. Luckily a daily ferry crosses the St. Johns River between the parking lot and the island. Of special interest is a 300-foot-long Timucuan Indian ceremonial mound. No vehicles allowed. Besides being a sanctuary for the endangered bald eagle, this is a good place to fish, picnic and

camp in either tents or cabins. The park is open 8:00
A.M.—sunset daily year-round. Six miles west of De Land off
SR 44; (904) 736–5309.

Between Sanford and Longwood keep an eye out for the
Big Tree marker. The country's largest bald cypress tree is
less than a mile up the cutoff road. "The Senator" is 126 feet
high with a diameter of 17 1/2 feet and an estimated age of
more than 3,000 years. Impressive! Big Tree Park is on General Hutchinson Parkway, Longwood, Florida. The Seminole
County Parks and Recreation department closes the gates at
sunset. Free.

You are not going to believe there are this many cacti in
the world until you tour the greenhouses at Florida Cactus,
Inc. in Plymouth. Is your idea of a cactus green? Take a good
long look at the endless rows of red, yellow and pink cacti.
Six thousand cacti make up a large (24 by 12 feet) map of the
United States in which each state features a different variety
of cactus. Wondering what time it is? Check the electric clock
made up of 12,000 cacti. The time is not hard to read as the
clock is 75 feet in circumference.

You may buy (or just admire) dish gardens, colorful graft-
ed cacti, cactus books and a special fertilizer called "Granny's
cactus juice." The mailing address is Florida Cactus, Inc., P.O.
Box 2900, Apopka, FL 32704. The greenhouse, at S. Peterson
Road in Plymouth, Florida, is off U.S. 441. Turn off 441 onto
Boy Scout Boulevard. Follow the Florida Cactus signs to
South Peterson Road. Open 7:30 A.M.—5:00 P.M. Monday
through Friday, and 7:30—11:30 A.M. on Saturday, closed
Sunday; (407) 886–1833.

Orlando Area

The Maitland Art Center is a special place. Originally
designed to be a retreat for avant garde artists, it is now an
attractive complex housing a fascinating permanent collection and monthly rotating exhibits by contemporary artists.
The buildings, adorned with murals and ornamental carvings
in Aztec-Mayan motif, are well worth seeing, as is the tranquil garden and courtyard area. When you visit the Garden
Chapel with its trellised walkway, you'll understand why this

is such a popular place for weddings. Maitland Art Center, 231 W. Packwood Avenue, Maitland, FL 32751. Open 10:00 A.M.—4:00 P.M. Monday through Friday, 1:00—4:00 P.M. on Saturday and Sunday. Call (407) 645–2181. Free.

If you love birds, you'll be very happy at the Audubon House, which includes a gallery, a large collection of live birds in an aviary and a gift shop featuring books on birds and recordings of bird calls. Its Center for Birds of Prey is one of the leading raptor rehabilitation centers in the state. You are encouraged to report injured or orphaned birds of prey to (407) 647–2615 during business hours or to (407) 645–3826 weekends and evenings. Audubon House is at 1101 Audubon Way, Maitland, FL 32751. Open Monday through Friday 10:00 A.M.—4:00 P.M., Saturday 10:00 A.M.—2:00 P.M. The aviary is closed on Monday. Call (407) 647–2615.

Winter Park is an elegant, if hard to park in, little college town with plenty of interesting things to see and do. Shoppers will find Park Avenue bristling with expensive boutiques and fine restaurants. Don't miss the crystal and fine art displayed at the Center Street Gallery at 136 S. Park Avenue. Open 9:30 A.M.—5:30 P.M. Monday through Saturday.

The largest collection of Tiffany glass and jewelry in the world resides at the Morse Gallery of Art in Winter Park. This small gallery features late nineteenth- and twentieth-century art and decorative arts including leaded stained glass windows, lamps, blown glass, pottery, paintings and furniture. Tiffany admirers will want a copy of the beautiful book titled *The 'Lost' Treasures of Louis Tiffany* (published by Doubleday in 1980) by the gallery's director, Hugh McKean, which provides some insight into Tiffany art. Open Tuesday through Saturday 9:30 A.M.—4:00 P.M. and Sunday 1:00—4:00 P.M. The Morse Gallery of Art, 133 E. Welbourne Avenue, Winter Park, FL 32789; (407) 644–3638.

Winter Park's Rollins College has a beautiful campus with even more going for it than the attractive Spanish/Mediterranean architecture. The college's Cornell Fine Arts Center with three galleries of rotating art exhibits is open to the public year-round 10:00 A.M.—5:00 P.M. Tuesday through Friday and 1:00—5:00 P.M. Saturday and Sunday; (407) 646–2526.

One fun way to really appreciate this lovely lake-dotted area is to take a **Scenic Boat Tour.** The boat leaves from the eastern foot of Morse Boulevard on Lake Osceola in Winter Park. The one-hour narrated ride takes you through various Winter Park lakes and canals, by estates, the Isle of Sicily, Kraft Azalea Gardens and Rollins College. Scenic Boat Tour, Lake Osceola, Winter Park, FL 32789. Daily 10:00 A.M.—4:30 P.M.; (407) 644-4056.

Central Florida's major city, Orlando, was settled by soldiers who decided to stick around after the Seminole wars in the 1830s. It was little more than a cattle country trading post until the railroad's arrival brought an influx of people and business in 1880. Then the town eased into a string of unremarkable years as a shipping center for citrus fruits and vegetables.

Over the years, Orlando capitalized on its best features—fifty-four lakes within the city limits and a year-round average temperature of 72 degrees. The community protected its venerable groves of live oaks by creating forty-seven parks. A loyal contingent of northerners who appreciated both the beauty and the climate enjoyed the town's relaxed pace each winter.

Those were the days before the nation's launch into space from nearby Cape Canaveral and before the coming of Walt Disney World. The city is still pretty with all its lakes and parks intact, but the relaxed pace is a memory. Orlando is one of the fastest growing metropolitan areas in the United States, and the face of Central Florida has been forever changed.

Even folks in Liechtenstein know about Orlando. But they don't know all about it, because there is lots going on that's not even remotely connected to Mickey Mouse. You're welcome, for example, to attend the **U. S. Navy Recruit Graduation Exercises** held each Friday morning at 9:45. The Navy pulls out all the stops, and the colorful ceremony includes the Navy Band, the famous Bluejacket chorus, precision drill teams and the fifty-state flag team to mark the graduation of Navy men and women from boot camp. Guaranteed to rouse your patriotic feelings, this stirring event takes place off E. Colonial Drive in Orlando; (407) 646-4522.

Loch Haven Park in Orlando offers a cluster of quality attractions. Parking is easy, and you may spend all day enjoying the Orlando Museum of Art, Orange County Historical Museum and Orlando Science Center. The Art Center has a growing permanent collection of twentieth-century American art, pre-Columbian artifacts, African art and changing exhibitions from internationally renowned museums and private collections. Gallery hours are 9:00 A.M.—5:00 P.M. Tuesday through Thursday; 9:00 A.M.—9:00 P.M. Friday; 10:00 A.M.—5:00 P.M. Saturday; noon—5:00 P.M. Sunday. (407) 896–4231. Free.

The Orange County Historical Museum began in 1942 when a group of women set up a pioneer kitchen in the 1892 red brick courthouse for a country-wide centennial. It has evolved into a handsome museum that will take you on a trip down memory lane. Here you'll travel back to the time when Florida was a wilderness, learn about the Big Freeze of 1894—95 that destroyed the citrus industry and ride the roller coaster real estate boom-and-bust days of the 1920s. On display are a 1,000-year-old Timucuan Indian canoe, a newspaper composing room in the hot type tradition, a Victorian parlor and the hide of a 15-foot alligator. Open Tuesday through Friday 9:00 A.M.—5:00 P.M., Saturday and Sunday noon—5:00 P.M. Orange County Historical Museum, Loch Haven Park, 812 East Rollins Street, Orlando, FL 32803; (407) 898–8320.

Out the back door you'll find Fire Station No. 3, Orlando's oldest standing firehouse, which operates as an extension of the Historical Museum. This captures the flavor of the early bucket brigade days and comes complete with a traditional sliding pole, an 1885 hose cart and even a potbellied stove. It's open Wednesday, Thursday and Friday 10:00 A.M.—4:00 P.M., noon—5:00 P.M. Saturday and Sunday; (407) 898–8320.

Those who find their earth weight discouraging may take consolation in learning their moon weight, one of many neat things you can do at the Orlando Science Center. A computer will ask you a lot of questions and use the answers to come up with your risk of having a heart attack. You can produce your own electricity by riding a bike or buy freeze-dried astronaut ice cream. This is one of those places where you learn a great deal while having a good time, and it is especially good for families. Ask about the daily planetarium shows. Open Monday through Thursday 9:00 A.M.—5:00 P.M., Friday 9:00 A.M.—9:00 P.M., Saturday noon—9:00 P.M. and Sunday noon—5:00 P.M. Orlando Science Center and John

Young Planetarium, Loch Haven Park, 810 E. Rollins Street, Orlando, FL 32803; (407) 896–7151.

When the hustle and bustle of Orlando is too much with you, a walk through Leu Gardens provides a welcome tonic. More than 50 acres of trees, flowering shrubs, roses, camellias, orchids and azaleas border Lake Rowena. Several floral varieties bloom most of the year, but the big show is from December to March as this is primarily a winter garden. A museum house, which shows how a well-to-do Florida family lived at the turn-of-the-century, is open Tuesday through Saturday 10:00 A.M.—3:30 P.M., Sunday and Monday 1:00—3:30 P.M. Tours on the half hour. Leu House and Gardens, 1730 N. Forest Avenue, Orlando, FL 32803; (407) 894–6021.

Camping sounds like fun, but you want a real vacation complete with daily maid service, cable TV and air conditioning. Surprise! You can have it all at **Walt Disney World's Fort Wilderness Campground.** More than 350 Fleetwood trailers are fully equipped with dishes and cooking utensils and dishwashers. Most sleep six. While enjoying all the comforts and conveniences of a fine hotel, you can also have the rustic beauty of the Great Outdoors.

Hearty fare and wholesome fun is close by. The Hoop-Dee-Doo-Revue at Pioneer Hall is the second-longest-running show at Walt Disney World. A cast of six "stagecoach passengers" keeps everyone in stitches for almost two hours. In between laughs, fill up on fried chicken, barbecued ribs, corn on the cob and strawberry shortcake. After, it's home-sweet-home to your trailer under the trees. For information about Fort Wilderness, write Walt Disney World Central Reservations, P.O. Box 40, Lake Buena Vista, FL 32830, or call (407) 824–8000.

Just in case you're in the mood for an early morning hot air balloon ride over Orlando, Church Street Station is standing by. Start the day with coffee and orange juice and polish off your aerial adventure with a champagne brunch at Lili Marlene's Restaurant. A day to store in the memory forever! Call (407) 422–2434.

Church Street Station also features Phineas Phogg's Balloon Works (purveyors of balloons, burgers and boogie), Apple Annie's Courtyard, and Cheyenne Saloon and Opera House. Nickel beer night is on Wednesdays, and western and

Indian antiques are available at Buffalo Trading Co. It's impossible to take advantage of all the excitement at Church Street Station, but you might as well try. This complete dining, shopping and entertainment complex is open every day 11:00 A.M.—2:00 P.M. and features twenty live shows nightly. Church Street Station is at 129 W. Church Street, Orlando, FL 32801; (407) 422–2434.

Places of Learning is a lot more fun than it sounds. Imagine a map of the United States that covers an entire acre (an inch equals a mile). Hike the entire Lewis and Clark trail as well as other famous routes of exploration in high heels if you wish. Be careful, because the Great Lakes are actual bodies of water. Pick out your state flag, walk through a giant chess game the size of half a tennis court and read a few pages from fifteen famous children's classics that are five feet high and eight feet wide.

Places of Learning is all free, but the wonderful selection of children's books and games in The Parent's Store is hard to resist. At any time of year, it's a great place to do your Christmas and birthday shopping. Don't leave The Parent's Store without trying your hand at one of the computer quizzes. Places of Learning is the brainchild of Harcourt Brace Jovanovich Inc., one of the world's largest publishers. Open daily 9:00 A.M.—7:00 P.M. Places of Learning, 6825 Academic Drive, Orlando, FL 32821; (407) 345–1038. Free.

The place to get a king-size inferiority complex about the state of your kitchen cupboards is Tupperware World Headquarters. These folks give a fine tour, which includes pictorial displays of the manufacturing process, a lovely home setting where you'll see every imaginable use for Tupperware and a museum of historic food containers that date as far back as 4000 B.C. Makes you feel grateful for leftovers! The building and grounds are splendid, especially the circular fountain, which is a replica of the famous King's Cross Fountain in Sydney, Australia. A small Tupperware gift concludes the half-hour tour. Tupperware World Headquarters, U.S. 441, Kissimmee, FL. Open 8:30 A.M.—-5:00 P.M. Monday through Friday; (407) 847–3111. Free.

While you're in the neighborhood, **Gatorland Zoo** (next door to Tupperware) should be in your plans. Don't worry about the huge alligator jaws you walk through to enter.

This isn't just another hokey attraction, but a fine zoo with more than 4,000 alligators and crocodiles (Gatorland claims to be the world's largest alligator farm attraction) and some rather exotic animals including snakes, birds, monkeys and a perfectly lovely tapir. An interesting artificial insemination program for alligators is in full swing here.

Allow plenty of time to stroll the boardwalk through the eerie beauty of a cypress swamp. This sanctuary, lush with wild orchids and ferns, offers a welcome reprieve from the hectic pace some sightseers set for themselves. Open daily 8:00 A.M.—8:00 P.M. (8:00 A.M.—6:00 P.M. during the winter), Gatorland is on U.S. 441 next to Tupperware. Mailing address: 14501 S. Orange Blossom Terrace, Orlando, FL 32821; (407) 857–3845.

A novel way to see the "real" Florida is by piloting your own airboat. Explore wild cypress swamps where tall waterbirds stalk their supper and trees are festooned with Spanish moss. You'll get the hang of the steering bar right away. Just pull back if you want to go right and push forward to go left. Only ten minutes from Walt Disney World, this lovely natural spot can also be seen by electric boat and/or canoe. Boats and canoes can be rented at Airboat Rentals U-Drive, which is 6 miles east of I-4 on U.S. 192 in Kissimmee; (407) 847–3672.

Aaah, the romance of Medieval Times when brave knights defended their kingdoms and castles were scenes of great feasts and much revelry. This is now a possible dream thanks to **Medieval Times Dinner Tournament.** Slip back to Europe in the eleventh century and admire valiant knights on richly attired horses. A "serving wench" brings a delicious four-course dinner, which you eat with your hands. (Remember this is the year of grace 1092.)

Spectacular pageantry, splendid horses galloping at full tilt and knights who duel to the death (well, almost) combine to make quite an evening. Just when you thought chivalry was dead, a knight shows up and throws you a flower. A knight to remember! Medieval Times is on U. S. 192 in Kissimmee. Medieval Times, P. O. Box 422385, Kissimmee, FL 34742. Toll-free in Florida: 1–800–432–0768; toll-free nationwide: 1–800–327–4024. The number for the castle in Kissimmee is (407) 396–1518.

For a look into the "Home of the Future," take a leisurely

electronic tour through Xanadu, where the twenty-first century is in full swing. Computers choose the menu (according to your nutritional needs), cook the food and clean up. This house is energy efficient and climate controlled, and boasts a waterfall spa that looks like all kinds of fun. Made of rigid polyurethane and resembling a rambling white space ship, the house has fifteen rooms. Open daily 10:00 A.M.—10:00 P.M., Xanadu, P.O. Box 2286, Kissimmee, FL 32741, is at the intersection of U. S. 192 and SR 535; (407) 396–1992.

Kissimmee had a long proud heritage as capital of cattle country before being billed as the Gateway to Walt Disney World. Spanish explorers brought livestock to the New World, and when Florida became a United States territory in 1821, the open range and scrub cattle descended from Spanish cows lured homesteaders to the Florida frontier. South of Orlando's dazzle, hundreds of cattle ranches and a thriving beef and dairy industry prosper. The cowboy's own brand of excitement rears up twice a year at Florida's largest and oldest professional rodeo, Kissimmee's Silver Spurs. For information about these special events or about attending a weekly cattle auction (Wednesdays) contact the Kissimmee—St. Cloud Convention and Visitors Bureau, P. O. Box 422007, Kissimmee, FL 32742-2007; 1–800–432–9199 (in Florida) or 1–800–327–9159.

In Kissimmee, don't forget to visit the Monument of States, made of stones from every state in the Union. The 70-foot structure was built by Kissimmee citizens in 1943 with 1,500 stones from every state and twenty-one foreign countries. Near the lakefront in downtown Kissimmee.

Kissimmee lies at the head of the 50-mile-long **Kissimmee Chain-of-Lakes,** and those who want to experience central Florida at its natural best should see it from the water. Far from the madding crowd are quiet lagoons and blue herons picking their way through water hyacinths. Besides being splendidly scenic, this is one of the country's best bass fishing grounds. The sunset is in living color, the view is multidimensional and the big sound is a night chorus of tree frogs and cicadas. Houseboats and assorted other craft may be rented on Lake Tohopekaliga. Take U. S. 192 to SR 17-92 south, then at the second or third traffic light, turn left to lakefront. For information, call Parks and Recreation; (407) 847–2388.

Originally founded in 1972 as a research center for the production and distribution of snake venoms, Reptile World Serpentarium now offers close-up views of poisonous snakes being milked. Time your visit to be on hand during one of three daily venom programs given at 11:00 A.M., 2:00 P.M. and 5:00 P.M. You'll see turtles and alligators as well as cobras, mambas, vipers, rattlesnakes and giant pythons. The gift shop has an excellent selection of books on reptiles. Open Tuesday through Sunday 9:00 A.M.—5:30 P.M. Closed the month of September. Located 4 miles east of St. Cloud on U. S. 441-192. Reptile World Serpentarium, 5705 E. Bronson Memorial Highway, St. Cloud, FL 32769; (407) 892–6905.

Central Heartland

The central heartland of Florida seems, from certain viewpoints, like a huge sprawling sea of orange trees. Tidy parallel rows of trees undulate off into the distance like dark green waves. In the midst of citrus country are modern packing plants and frozen juice processors well equipped to handle the huge harvest. Many highway fruit and juice stands cater to tourists intent on carrying some fresh Florida fruit home to their winter-bound northern friends. At Orange Ring you can sample a free glass of orange juice and purchase any number of goodies including orange butter and chocolate alligators. The packing plant, behind the gift shop, gives brief tours during the week. Orange Ring, P.O. Drawer 2107, Haines City, FL 33845; (813) 422–1938. On U.S. 27 north of Haines City.

Watch citrus candy being made in copper kettles at Davidson of Dundee Citrus Candy Factory on U.S. 27 in Dundee. Open daily 8:00 A.M.—7:00 P.M. (8:00 A.M.—6:00 P.M. during the summer), but candy is not made on weekends. Davidson of Dundee, P. O. Box 800, Dundee, FL 33838; (813) 439–1698.

At Donald Duck's Citrus World you may view an eighteen-minute film that explains citrus packing and processing. After the movie, enjoy a free cup of juice and browse the extensive gift shop. Open from Monday through Friday 9:00

A.M.—4:30 P.M., Saturday 10:00 A.M.—3:00 P.M., but the film is only shown on weekdays. Located on U.S. 27 north of Lake Wales; (813) 676–1411.

Cypress Gardens in Winter Haven has been a popular tourist destination for many years. The Pope family began extensive landscaping on the shores of Lake Eloise in the 1930s. In 1942 they enlivened the botanical beauty by adding ski shows. Amateur and professional photographers as well as movie makers are drawn to the gorgeous scenery, and spectators cheer the talented skiers' mastery of the newest tricks.

Yet, few travelers are aware of Animal Forest Zoological Park at Cypress Gardens, which was recently recognized by the highly respected American Association of Zoological Parks and Aquariums. Some exotic species that have difficulty reproducing in captivity have had successful births, including a two-toed sloth and a colubus monkey. Kids may ride a giant Aldabra tortoise in the "Critter Encounter."

Cypress Gardens also has the only permanent themed ice show in the southeast, *Classic Ice,* with performances several times a day. A special treat for visitors is a luncheon cruise on Lake Eloise. Open daily 9:00 A.M.—6:00 P.M. The gardens are 3 miles southeast of Winter Haven on Co. Rd. 540. Cypress Gardens, P.O. Box 1, Cypress Gardens, FL 33884; (813) 324–2111.

Chalet Suzanne Country Inn and Restaurant, in Lake Wales, opens itself up like the petals of a flower. First, you discover a tiny whimsical pastel village with its thirty rooms each decorated in different combinations of Swedish tile, Spanish ironwork and Moorish mosaics. Then sample some of the Chalet's famous romaine soup in the intimate Old World dining room. (No wonder this soup was chosen to go to the moon with the crew of Apollo 15.) Each place is set with fine china, perhaps German porcelain or elegant Limoges, and your view overlooks a private lake.

Then you come upon the Chapel where you can buy all manner of fine glassware and antiques, the Wine Dungeon, the Wreck Room, the Soup Cannery and a ceramic salon where Lilliana and Boz Birvis are turning out treasures. Chalet Suzanne is one surprise after another, and that, and the good taste with which everything is done, accounts for its success as well as its charm.

Gourmet Magazine labeled Chalet Suzanne food "glorious" and surely it is, but be warned that the prices are also glorious. If a glance at the lunch menu withers your wallet, ask for the soup and sandwich du jour (unlisted). That way you can treat yourself to a fine meal without taking out a new mortgage. Owned and operated by the Hinshaw family since 1931, Chalet Suzanne is between Cypress Gardens and Bok Tower Gardens just off U.S. 27 and 17A. Or come by plane and land on the 2,450-foot private airstrip. Chalet Suzanne, P.O. Box A C, Lake Wales, FL 33859; (813) 676–6011. Expensive. *Great*

The 128-acre **Bok Tower Gardens** in Lake Wales have been devoted to peace and beauty since 1928. Listed in the National Register of Historic Places, the gardens and tower were dedicated to the American people because Edward Bok, a Dutch immigrant, wanted to make America "a bit more beautiful" because he had lived here. The hushed atmosphere of the surroundings is interrupted only by a daily bell serenade (3:00 P.M.) from the 205-foot "singing" tower, which has been called one of the world's great carillons. Enjoy the azaleas, camellias, magnolias and many birds. Surrounded by citrus orchards, this is the place to come in the spring when the air is heavy with the scent of orange blossoms. The gardens are open every day 8:00 A.M.—5:00 P.M. Located 3 miles north of Lake Wales off Co. Rd. 17A (Burns Avenue). Bok Tower Gardens, Lake Wales, FL 33859–3810; (813) 676–1408.

Lake Kissimmee State Park is way off the beaten path, but worth it. The park consists of more than 5,000 acres bordered by lakes Kissimmee, Tiger and Rosalie. The lakes, floodplain prairies, marshes and pine flatwoods are home to a variety of wildlife including the rare Florida panther. (Don't count on seeing a panther; they're very shy.) This is a fine spot to boat, hike, picnic and camp. For an excellent view of Lake Kissimmee, try the top of the observation platform.

One of the best features of the park is a reconstructed **1876 cow camp** with scrub cows and "cow hunters." (They will quickly tell you they do not care to be called cowboys.) Here you can learn firsthand about the bustling cattle business on the south Florida frontier, and see one of the few remaining herds of scrub cows in existence.

As you walk down the trail to the camp, you travel back to the year 1876. The cow hunter may be having a cup of cof-

Bok Tower

fee near his campfire, or perhaps is rounding up cows for the long cattle drive to the west coast of Florida. The cattlemen were paid in gold Spanish doubloons. The cow hunter welcomes your questions, but don't bother asking about anything that happened after 1876. He will just look very puzzled and won't know what you're talking about.

The cow camp is only open on weekends and holidays from 9:30 A.M.—4:30 P.M. The park is open daily 7:00 A.M.—sunset year-round. Lake Kissimmee State Park, 14248 Camp Mack Road, Lake Wales, FL 33853. The park is 15 miles east of Lake Wales, off Camp Mack Road. Call (813) 696–1112.

Follow nature trails and boardwalks through the jungles, cypress swamps and tropical wilderness of **Highlands Hammock State Park.** Your stroll will be rewarded with glimpses of sunning alligators and rare orchids. You'll also want to visit the small museum and ride the park's "trackless train" on regularly scheduled wildlife tours. A good place to bike (rentals available), picnic and camp. Highland Hammocks is open daily 8:00 A.M. until sunset, 6 miles west of Sebring, off U. S. 27–98; (813) 385–0011.

Florida Southern College, in Lakeland, boasts the world's largest concentration of architecture by Frank Lloyd Wright. Wright's design for these seven unconventional buildings called for steel for strength, sand for Florida and glass to bring the outdoors in. The steeple of the Annie Pfeiffer Chapel, designed as a chime resonator, casts shifting shadows into the interior. Tinted glass squares filter colored light in during the day. The low esplanade, a sheltered walkway, was obviously not designed with today's basketball players in mind; no ceiling or doorway is much over six feet tall! The Science Building, more than 400 feet long with a planetarium at the southern end, is the largest structure, and some say the most magnificent.

The lakeside campus is open to the public 8:00 A.M.—5:00 P.M. weekdays. Pick up a map for a self-guided tour in the Administration Building. Florida Southern College, Lakeland, FL 33801-5698; (813) 680–4111. From Orlando, go west on I-4 to U.S. 98 exit. Turn right on U. S. 98 to Memorial Boulevard. Left on Memorial Boulevard to Ingraham Avenue. Turn right, stay on Ingraham until reaching the campus. Free.

Ocala Area

The Ocala area is a land of gently rolling hills, massive oaks bearded with Spanish moss and sleek thoroughbreds gamboling in neatly fenced paddocks. This is the fastest growing thoroughbred community in the world and is responsible for Florida's development, in less than half a century, as a major force in international racing and breeding.

The racing world sat up and took notice when Needles became the first Florida-bred to win the Kentucky Derby in 1956. Since then what started as a few converted cattle farms has grown to nearly 500 thoroughbred facilities. Marion County is now second only to Lexington, Kentucky, in concentration of **thoroughbred farms.**

Central Florida offers ideal conditions for raising superior thoroughbreds. Year-round sunshine, mineral-rich water and fertile pastureland have turned out to be a winning combination. Mild weather, with cold snaps rarely lasting more than a few days, plays an important role. Central Florida's extended springs and autumns flank a long summer. The absence of a harsh winter means that, rather than standing idle in their stalls, horses run free all year. Unlike its northern counterpart, a new Florida foal is usually out romping with its dam within hours of its birth.

The area is wonderfully scenic, and many horse farms welcome visitors for self-guided tours, but the hours vary. Visitors are encouraged to pick up information at the Ocala/Marion Chamber of Commerce on 110 E. Silver Springs Road, Ocala; or call (904) 629–8051; or write P. O. Box 1210, Ocala, FL 32678.

Just east of Ocala is the **Ocala National Forest** with more than 300,000 acres of untamed springs, winding streams and natural lakes. The southernmost national forest in the continental United States, Ocala is a popular recreation area for canoeing, swimming, camping, hiking, picnicking and hunting. Detailed maps of the forest may be obtained at the two ranger stations. USDA Forest Service, 227 N. Bronough Street, Suite 4061, Tallahassee, FL 32301. (904) 681–7265.

While this is the largest area of sand pine in the world with one of the largest deer herds in Florida, it is the clear, clean springs that steal the show. Alexander Springs pumps out seventy-six million gallons of 72-degree water each day of the year. The spring here is so large that local scuba experts use it for new diver certification tests. Canoers use this run for an excursion into the unspoiled forest, and swimmers and sunbathers make good use of the large sand beach. Located in Ocala National Forest off Co. Rd. 445.

Another favorite, Juniper Springs, contributes 20 million gallons to the local water supply. Besides swimming, the most popular activity is canoeing the seven-mile spring run. This campground is in such demand that reservations are not accepted, and accommodations are handled on a first-come basis. Located in Ocala National Forest on SR 40 just west of SR 19.

Salt Springs Recreation Area is on the shores of a beautiful natural spring, which empties into Lake George, the state's second largest lake. The five-mile spring run is ideal for canoeing, boating and fishing; the spring boil is a mecca for swimmers and snorkelers. Located in Ocala National Forest on SR 19 about 16 miles north of SR 40, Salt Springs has complete camping facilities; (904) 685–2048.

Silver Glen Springs is a beautiful 1,000-acre camping area bordering a crystal clear spring. A good place to bird-watch, swim, boat or fish. Located in Ocala National Forest off U. S. 19, 6 miles north of SR 40; (904) 685–2514.

While Ocala's waterworks are impressive, they are literally just a drop in the region's overflowing bucket. Of the country's seventy-eight major springs, twenty-seven are in Florida. Its central section is literally riddled with them. Springs are classified according to volume—a major spring, one of first magnitude, produces 100 cubic feet of water a second or more than sixty-four million gallons daily. The combined output from all 300 of Florida's known springs is eight billion gallons of water a day!

Silver Springs, near Ocala, is the largest limestone artesian spring formation in the world. With an average output of 800 million gallons a day, the springs have the greatest long-term measured average flow of any freshwater group in Florida. No wonder early Indians considered them sacred and paid homage to them with elaborate ceremonies. Scientists have discovered evidence of human activity dating back a hundred centuries. Certainly, this is one of Florida's oldest attractions.

Most of the earliest sightseers came by boat, although the 136-mile trip from Palatka involved several weeks poling along the tortuous Ocklawaha River. By the 1880s steamboats began regular trips from Palatka to the Springs carrying such notables as Mary Todd Lincoln, Harriet Beecher Stowe and William Cullen Bryant. The expedition, a real breeze, took only two nights and a day.

Visitors are rarely disappointed in this natural wonder. The limestone-filtered water in the deep blue pool inspired one early journalist to describe the springs as shining "like an enormous jewel." Phillip Morrell, a young man living at Silver Springs, invented the glass bottom boat to provide passengers their first fish-eye view of the aquatic world. Watching this everchanging panorama while gliding over the pellucid springs is still a favorite activity. Numerous movies and television shows, attracted by the extraordinary clarity, have done underwater filming in this location.

The luxuriant gardens and subtropical scenery on the 100-acre site add to the viewing pleasure. Other diversions at the springs include a classic car collection, a deer park, reptile demonstrations and a jungle cruise past a whole zoo's worth of exotic animals. You'll see giraffes, ostriches, camels and a colony of monkeys descended from those used in the old Tarzan movies. Located just off I-75, one mile east of Ocala on SR 40. Open daily 9:00 A.M.—5:30 P.M. Florida's Silver Springs, P. O. Box 370, Silver Springs, FL 32688; (904) 236–2121.

Western Interior

You'll get your exercise if you cover all 40 acres of canopies, stalls and sheds at Webster Flea Market, one of the largest flea markets in the Southeast. It's hard to believe this all started in 1937 as a one-shed farmers' produce auction. More than 1,500 vendors await you and your spare change. It's all here—from fine antiques, fresh produce and homemade sausage to just plain junk. You'll be exhausted if you try to see everything there is to see, but you'll surely find at least one item you cannot live another day without. Open every Monday 9:00 A.M.—3:30 P.M. Webster Flea Market, P. O.

Box 62, Highway 471, Webster, FL 33597; (904) 793–2021.

The Dade Battlefield State Historic Site is the picture of serenity now, but it was once drenched in blood. Here Indians, who were not pleased at the prospect of being evicted from their land, ambushed more than 100 soldiers under the command of Maj. Francis L. Dade. The Dade Massacre, as it came to be known, touched off the Second Seminole War, a war that dragged on for seven years and became the country's costliest Indian war. While visiting the small museum and reading the markers along the nature trail, you'll have a chance to ponder the events of December 28, 1835. Dade Battlefield Historic Site, P. O. Box 938, Bushnell, FL 33513. Located southwest of Bushnell off U. S. 301; (904) 793–4781.

Gulf Coast *We like this place—Manatees*

If you haven't looked a manatee in the eye lately, you will never have a better opportunity than at **Homosassa Springs Wildlife Park.** You may pay a visit to these gentle mammals while walking under water (and staying nice and dry) at Fish Bowl Spring.

Besides the lovable manatees, you'll see more than thirty-four varieties of fish, both saltwater and freshwater species. Feeding time at Gator Lagoon will cure you of thinking you can outswim a hungry gator. A fish is hooked to a wire and skimmed across the pool with alligators in hot pursuit. Wow! Be sure to take the nature cruise, stroll the trails and feed the deer in the petting zoo. Located just west of U. S. 19. Homosassa Springs, P. O. Box 189, Homosassa Springs, FL 32647; (904) 628–2311.

Yulee Sugar Mill Ruins State Historic Site was once part of a thriving sugar plantation, the area's first known settlement made by a white man. David Yulee, a former U. S. Senator, operated the mill for thirteen years beginning in 1951. He supplied the Confederate Army with sugar products until 1864 when a Union naval force burned Yulee's home to the ground. Interpretive signs will guide you through the partially restored sugar mill, the only antebellum structure of its kind in the country. Located in Homosassa on SR 490 southwest of U. S. 19. Write to Yulee Sugar Mill Ruins, c/o Crystal

River State Archaeological Site, Rte. 3, Box 610, Crystal River, FL 32629; (904) 795–3817.

And you thought Christmas came only once a year. Not at Roger's Christmas House and Village, which is open every day except December 25th. You're welcome to browse the ten rooms of the Christmas House, which overflow with trees, wreaths, gifts and the widest selection of ornaments in the country. Before long, you are feeling festive. Next to the original house are Country Cottage, Magnolia House, Little House Under the Oak Tree and Storybook Land with animated display figures. Open daily 9:30 A.M.—5:00 P.M. One block from the intersection of U. S. 98, SR 50 and U. S. 41. Roger's Christmas House, 103 Saxon Avenue, P. O. Box 1267, Brooksville, FL 34601; (904) 796–2415.

Weeki Wachee Springs is home to live mermaids as well as more traditional denizens of the deep. The unusual theatre is 16 feet below the surface of the spring (which is more than 137 feet deep) with glass windows for your viewing pleasure. Walk through lush tropical gardens and ride a Wilderness River Cruise Boat, which passes the Pelican Orphanage, a refuge for disabled sea birds. Don't miss the exotic bird show or the impressive performance by no-nonsense birds of prey. Weeki Wachee Springs, Box 97, Weeki Wachee, FL 34605. The theme park is on U.S. 19 South at the junction of SR 50; (904) 596–2062.

Tarpon Springs' famous sponge industry began in the 1890s when John K. Cheyney launched his first sponge-fishing boat and began hooking sponges. In 1905 John Cocoris, a recent immigrant from Greece, introduced the diving techniques used to harvest sponges in the Mediterranean. The first Tarpon Springs sponger to try this method emerged after a ten-minute dive thoroughly convinced that these sponge beds could supply the whole world.

Word of the bountiful beds off Tarpon Springs spread to Greece, and soon whole families were packing up their lives and moving to the west coast of Florida. From their homeland they brought the colorful customs and traditional cuisine of the rich Hellenic Culture.

The village prospered during the first forty years of the twentieth century as sponging grew to be a multi-million dollar business. Auctions held at the Sponge Exchange were lively affairs, and Tarpon Springs soon surpassed Key West as the country's main sponging center. But in the 1940s a mysterious disease known as the red tide decimated the sponge beds, and consumers began turning to synthetic sponges.

Today visitors fascinated by this Greek community stroll the sponge docks, which have been designated a National Historic Landmark. The Sponge Exchange has been taken over by boutiques and gift shops, but a few boats still return from sea with ropes of sponges drying in the rigging. The history of the sponge industry is recounted at Spongeorama Exhibit Center, and visitors may join a half-hour cruise featuring a sponge diving demonstration by a copper-helmeted diver.

Lining the docks are many Greek coffeehouses and restaurants where a meal of pastitso and baklava may be washed down with a glass of retsina wine. The Spongeorama Exhibit Center is at 510 Dodecanese Boulevard at the Sponge Docks; (813) 942–3771. Information on Tarpon Springs is available at the Greater Tarpon Springs Chamber of Commerce, 528 E. Tarpon Avenue, Tarpon Springs, FL 33589; (813) 937–6109.

The community still revolves around the church. St. Nicholas Greek Orthodox Cathedral, a fine example of neobyzantine architecture with icons, stained glass and sculptured marble, was named for the patron saint of ships and seafaring men. The celebration of Epiphany held each January 6th is a study in pomp and pageantry. The archbishop leads the colorful procession from the church to Spring Bayou, the site of the original settlement. There he releases a dove and tosses a large gold cross into the water. Young men dive for the sacred trophy, and the successful one receives a blessing, which is supposed to bring him a year of good luck. The community then funnels all its energies into singing and dancing. Especially during this Old World festival, Tarpon Springs seems more like a Mediterranean community than a Floridian one. The church is at 35 N. Pinellas Avenue; (813) 937–3540.

Tampa—St. Petersburg Area

Spanish explorers discovered Tampa in the sixteenth century. They also discovered the resident Indians who resisted being converted to Catholicism and resented the European urge for conquering. The resulting clash of interests led to bloodshed frequently over the years. Approximately 300 years later in 1824 the Americans built Fort Brooke in an effort to subdue the Seminoles.

But the city's real development didn't begin until 1883 when Henry B. Plant linked Tampa with Jacksonville by a combination of railroad and steamship connections. As if to confirm Plant's faith in the city's future, Vincente Martinez Ybor, who was having labor problems in Key West and was attracted by Tampa's lower taxes, moved his cigar factory here in 1886. Most of the cigar-making community came with him.

If you'd like to see cigars made by the old hand rolling method as well as by modern machine, Villazon and Company gives half-hour tours Monday through Friday at 9:30 A.M. After the tour, gentlemen are given a sample of the product. Closed holidays and several weeks in midsummer. Villazon & Company, 3104 N. Armenia, Tampa, FL 33607; (813) 879–2291. Free.

Henry Plant, competing with East Coast railroad tycoon Henry Flagler, erected the ostentatious Moorish-style Tampa Bay Hotel in 1891. Sporting silver Turkish minarets, the palatial hotel ushered in Tampa's era as a fashionable winter resort for well-heeled northerners. Costing a cool $3.5 million, it was regarded in its day as the most elegant and most expensive hotel in the world.

Today, it is considered the finest example of Moorish architecture in the Western Hemisphere and is home to the University of Tampa. To see some of the furniture and art of the late Victorian era, visit the Henry B. Plant Museum in a wing of the main university building. Open Tuesday through Saturday. The hotel/university is on John F. Kennedy Boulevard at the Hillsborough River; (813) 253–6231. Museum and guided walking tours (ask for schedule) are free.

Today, Tampa is a major industrial metropolis and busy shipping center for a great variety of products including phosphates, citrus fruits and cattle. At day's end, you may be interested in watching shrimp boats unload their catch at the shrimp docks on the Twenty-second Street Causeway. Free.

Citizens have worked hard to preserve Tampa's heritage. The Hispanic community centered in **Ybor City** has been largely returned to its late nineteenth-century appearance. Cigar makers demonstrate the art of hand rolling in restored **Ybor Square,** a complex of shops and restaurants. Ybor City, which is a National Historic District, is bounded by Columbus Drive, Fifth Avenue, Nebraska Avenue and Twenty-second Street.

Around the turn of the century, the Ferlita Bakery flourished along with Ybor City and the cigar industry. In the "Cigar Capital of the World" workers lived very well indeed, and a "boom town" atmosphere prevailed. The bakery (listed on the National Register of Historic Sites) has now been transformed by the state of Florida into a museum where you can learn about Tampa's Latin community and see old photos, cigar industry artifacts and the original 1896 bakery oven. The Ybor City State Museum, 1818 Ninth Avenue, Tampa, FL 33605. Open 9:00 A.M.—noon and 1:00—5:00 P.M. Tuesday through Saturday. (813) 247–6323.

Tampa's distinct Latin flavor is retained in its Spanish shops, restaurants and the general ambiance of the community. You may see long loaves of Cuban bread rolled out by hand at La Segunda Central Bakery if you arrive before 9:00 A.M. Go around to the back door and watch as bakers shape the dough and place a single strand of palmetto leaf on each yard-long loaf. The bakery is at 2515 Fifteenth Street in Ybor City.

You may buy a fresh loaf from the store, or order a Cuban sandwich (looking for all the world like a sub) for lunch at a number of Spanish restaurants on E. Seventh Street in Ybor City. If you choose La Tropicana, you'll notice one table in the back that looks different from all the rest. It even has its own old-fashioned upright phone used to gather news for the local scandal sheet. If you have something to contribute, stop in at La Tropicana at 1822 E. Seventh Street. While there, note the giant loaf of Cuban bread mounted very much like a prize fish over the counter. Those who don't go for subs might like the deviled crab or potato stuffed with meat. Both are very good and cost less than a dollar.

There's always a possibility you'll get caught in a hurricane, but then that's all part of the fun (and learning) going on at the Museum of Science and Industry. Take part in all kinds of fascinating experiments in this hands-on center and, whatever you do, don't miss Dr. Thunder's Magic Boom

Room. Exhibits and demonstrations explain the major scientific phenomena and industries of Florida—energy, weather, electricity, water, the environment, phosphate, agriculture and tourism. Recently expanded with many new things to see and do, the museum is in North Tampa 3 miles east of I-275 and is open daily 9:30 A.M.—4:30 P.M. Museum of Science and Industry, 4801 E. Fowler Avenue, Tampa, FL 33617; (813) 985–5531.

Get out your skateboard. Put on your jogging shoes or your roller skates. Tampa boasts nothing less than the longest continuous sidewalk in the world. Bayshore Boulevard's 6 1/2-mile sidewalk is the focus of much activity as folks take advantage of this scenic stretch bordering one of the city's oldest and finest residential areas. During a hurricane, this is where the water comes ashore and daring surfers replace joggers and skaters. You don't have to be quite that adventurous, but this just might be a good time to find out what it feels like to walk half a dozen miles.

One of the interesting things you'll see along Bayshore Boulevard is the *Jose Gasparilla,* the world's only fully rigged pirate ship. The ship stars during the annual Gasparilla Invasion held each February when businessmen-turned-buccaneers take over. The mayor officially surrenders the city, but apparently doesn't feel too bad about it, as he immediately declares a holiday to celebrate. The ensuing week-long festivities include torchlight parades, marathons and fancy dress balls. For information: The Greater Tampa Chamber of Commerce, 801 E. Kennedy Boulevard, P. O. Box 420, Tampa, FL 33601; (813) 228–7777.

You've seen grand palatial gardens before, but here's one that will be truly inspirational because it's done on a small, residential scale. You'll leave brimming with ideas for your own yard. Riverside Botanical Gardens is a half-acre garden displaying a large number of the palms, cycads, flowering trees and other interesting flora from around the world. You'll see a thorny Chorisia tree and Jamaican Red Banana, as well as a number of winged residents who think they own the place. Peacocks stroll the grounds, and the aviary by the river is abustle with all sorts of winged activity.

Don't be shy. This looks like a private residence because it is one, but owner William E. Field and landscape designer Brett Bachelor encourage visitors. The gardens are a mile northwest of downtown Tampa on the banks of the Hillsborough River. (Note: Two Riverside Drives appear on the map. Choose the one closest to downtown.) Open every day but Sunday 8:00 A.M.—4:00 P.M. Riverside Botanical Gardens, 2402 Riverside Drive, Tampa, FL 33602. Free.

You'll enjoy a "wild" safari on the African Serengiti Plain at Busch Gardens, the Dark Continent. Four hundred head of exotic big game including giraffes, zebras, elephants, gazelles and Cape buffalo roam at will as you cross the veldtlike plain via monorail, steam locomotive or skyride. Much more than an amusement park, Busch Gardens, with more than 3,000 animals, is regarded as one of the top four zoos in the country. Be sure to pay your respects to the rare white Bengal tigers and see Eagle Canyon, a newly constructed natural habitat display for American bald eagles and golden eagles located at the entrance to the Anheuser-Busch Brewery.

The brewery tour takes you inside a simulated beechwood aging tank, tells you all about the beer-making process and tops it all off with a nice cold sample. Busch Gardens (P.O. Box 9158, Tampa, FL 33674) is at 3000 Busch Boulevard, 2 miles east of I-275 and 2 miles west of I-75. Open daily 9:00 A.M.—8:00 P.M. except in summer and selected holidays when hours are extended. For a recorded message of operating hours and information call (813) 971–8282.

Bern's Steak House is as much an experience as it is a restaurant. The menu looks like an engineering spec sheet, the place is ornate (to put it mildly), and the emphasis is on doing things differently. Perhaps that explains why the gargantuan wine list is almost too heavy to lift. (To have your own copy, you'll have to part with more than $30. Don't try to walk off with one—it's chained to the table.)

From their own organic farm to the world's largest wine cellar, the emphasis at Bern's is on putting together the perfect meal. Waiters train a minimum of one year working in every station in the restaurant before being permitted in the dining room. Cress seeds from London are sprouted right in the kitchen and caviar is flown in daily. Your steak is cut, trimmed and weighed only after you have placed your order. Coffee beans are hand sorted and the whole operation is

71

coordinated by computer.

All this information (and much more) is on your menu, but is it all true? Yes. Bern's encourages tours of the kitchen and wine cellar throughout the evening. Between courses, diners take advantage of this offer to inspect the immaculate facilities and cavernous (and cold—take a sweater) wine cellar. They even get to see the sprouts sprouting.

The final course of coffee and dessert is served in your own private room upstairs, which comes complete with a color TV that you control. This way you can watch the restaurant musicians (and request a favorite song on your own phone) or choose from other TV entertainment. You may dance if you wish or simply spend the rest of the evening trying to select the perfect drink from a list of 1,000 dessert wines. The choice of dessert is not so overwhelming. Besides, you can't go wrong ordering Triple Chocolate. Bern's Steak House, 1208 S. Howard Avenue, Tampa, FL 33606; (813) 251-2421. In Florida: 1-800-282-1547. Expensive.

If there's a wee bit of Scottish in you, you'll be interested in knowing that Dunedin was founded by settlers from Scotland. The high school band's official uniform is the kilt, and the wail of bagpipes is a familiar sound at the festival Highland Games each March. Dunedin Scottish Imports is just the place to pick up bagpipe seasoning, potato scones or a stylish sporran. This amazing store/mail order business maintains the largest variety of tartan stock in the world, as well as black pudding, heather honey, ginger beer, Buchan thistle stoneware, kilt hose, meat pies and coarse cut marmalade. If it's Scottish, they probably have it. Dunedin Scottish Imports, 1251 Pinehurst Street, Dunedin, FL 33528; (813) 734-7606.

Take the scenic drive on Dunedin Beach Causeway to **Honeymoon Island State Recreation Area** and notice the large pines on the island's northern loop trail. This is one of a very few virgin slash pine stands in south Florida, as well as an important nesting site for the threatened osprey. A wide variety of plants and birds, including several endangered species, call this lovely island home. You may want to picnic, swim, fish or catch the ferry to Caladesi Island. Honeymoon Island is on SR 586 west of U.S. 19A; (813) 734-4255.

Caladesi Island, located off Dunedin, is one of Florida's few unspoiled barrier islands. Catch the ferry (which leaves hourly, weather permitting) from Dunedin Beach on Honeymoon Island and spend some time at this attractive state park. Accessible only by boat, this is a good place to swim, skin dive, boat, picnic or beachcomb for shells. The park has almost three miles of sandy beach, a ridge of virgin pine flatwoods and mangrove swamp. A 60-foot observation tower offers views of the area and of vessels in the Gulf. The island is north of Dunedin off U.S. 19A. For information call the ferry (813) 734–4134 or the park (813) 443–5903.

The **Kapok Tree Restaurant** in Clearwater is amazing. You really ought to see it even if you don't eat there. And you might as well eat there because the food is good and reasonably priced. First there's the Kapok tree, a native of India and Java. A few seeds were brought to this area by missionaries in the 1870s, but alas, only one survived. This is the remarkable survivor, and it is doing quite well, if 135 feet in height and 46 feet around the base is any indication. Before sprouting giant flame-colored blossoms in late February or early March, the tree drops all its leaves and looks like a goner.

The restaurant expanded around this unusual tree until it had eight dining rooms, numerous gift shops and a lounge. Allow plenty of time to roam the gardens. The East Garden fountains, a marvelous conglomeration of columns, statuary and cascading water, were inspired by the Villa d'Este near Rome. Inside huge crystal chandeliers and sculptured fountains seem to be everywhere. A wandering troubadour (in sixteenth-century dress) serenades diners on his dulcimer or flute. Can this really be Florida? Open at noon every day of the year, the Kapok Tree is at 923 McMullen-Booth Road, Clearwater, FL 33519; (813) 726–0504. Moderate.

Remember the old sugar cane mill, the railroad depot and the bandstand in the middle of the park? Open-air Heritage Park has these and more. Travel back in time to the early days of Pinellas County while browsing the old barn, church, cottage, loghouse and other structures. A guide in period dress will show you around, or you can poke about on your own. How did those early settlers manage? At least some of the answers are here in this pretty pine and palmetto park.

Open Tuesday through Saturday 10:00 A.M.—4:00 P.M., Sunday 1:00—4:00 P.M. Closed Monday. Heritage Park, 11909 125th Street North, Largo, FL 34644; (813) 462-3474. Free.

The **Suncoast Seabird Sanctuary** is dedicated to the rescue, repair, recuperation and, hopefully, the release of sick and injured wild birds. It all began when Ralph Heath nursed an injured cormorant back to health in 1971. Word spread and soon people were leaving injured birds on his doorstep. Today, the sanctuary is home to more than 500 birds and as many as twenty injured birds are brought daily. Unfortunately, more than 90 percent of these injuries are directly or indirectly related to human beings, who seem adept at throwing the delicate balance of nature out of kilter.

This nonprofit organization (supported entirely by donations) has a full-time staff of seven, a hospital complete with intensive-care room and an annual budget of $300,000. So far nearly 10,000 birds have been returned to the wild.

A recent success story involved the release of a southern bald eagle. Some permanently injured birds become full-time residents. You may watch endangered brown pelicans building nests with branches and rearing young in captivity. Notice the contingent of perfectly well birds perching on top of the wire cages. Isn't it thoughtful of them to visit their hospitalized friends?

Bring a camera and leave a donation or, better yet, fill out an application to adopt a bird. The sanctuary is open seven days a week from 9:00 A.M. until dark. Suncoast Seabird Sanctuary, 18328 Gulf Boulevard, Indian Shores, FL 34635; (813) 391-6211. Free.

A couple of sea turtle hunters returning from the Gulf were the first to see John's Pass in Madeira Beach. (It didn't exist until the hurricane of 1848.) Juan Levique was the one who spotted the changed coastline, so naturally it came to be known as John's Pass. Today, an early Florida fishing village atmosphere prevails. Boutiques and shops like Holy Shirt and the Fudge and Cookie Factory cater to tourists' whims. Choose from a large selection of beachwear, jewelry, stained glass or handcrafted items. This is a fine place to fish, charter a boat or just walk the boardwalk with an eye out for playful dolphins.

An excellent way to start the day is at the Friendly Fisherman Seafood Restaurant with a Boardwalk Breakfast. You can't miss with a basket of hot corn fritters. Later in the day, you can stop in and munch on grouper cheeks (no bones!). The Friendly Fisherman is on the boardwalk at John's Pass in Madeira Beach. Inexpensive.

No wonder folks flock to St. Petersburg with its exquisite beaches and 361 days of sunshine each year. Settled in the 1840s, St. Petersburg came to life in 1885 when Peter Demens extended his Orange Belt Railroad into the peninsula and named the settlement for his Russian birthplace. Imagine a place so confident of its sunshine that one of its newspapers gives away all the street editions if the weather remains cloudy for the entire day.

The world's largest collection of art by Spanish surrealist Salvador Dali can be found in St. Petersburg. The $35 million collection features oil paintings, watercolors, drawings, graphics and sculptures. The fascination here is to see Dali's development from 1914 to 1980. Open Tuesday through Saturday 10:00 A.M.—5:00 P.M. Sunday noon—5:00 P.M. Closed Monday. **The Salvador Dali Museum** is located in Poynter Park on the waterfront in south St. Petersburg at 1000 Third Street S., St. Petersburg, FL 33701; (813) 823–3767.

If you want a touch of history in your vacation itinerary, you will delight in the grand wedding cake of a hotel known as the Don Ce Sar. Take off your rose-colored glasses and it's still pink—really pink, as in flamingos, Easter eggs and bubble gum.

Unfortunately, a glorious opening night in January 1928 was followed by the stock market crash of 1929. Despite the patronage of such prominent guests as Scott and Zelda Fitzgerald, Clarence Darrow and Babe Ruth, the dismal days of the 1930s took their toll. Tourism had all but disappeared when the army bought it during the war for a song and turned it into a hospital. (The Bistro served as the morgue.) Deterioration and neglect pointed toward The Don's demise until a Save the Don committee worked a near miracle and rescued it during the 1970s.

The National Archives in Washington, D.C., lists the Don as

a historical monument, and it is one of three building landmarks used by the National Maritime Association on its maps and navigational aids for sailors. In April 1975, the Don was named to the National Register of Historic Places. An extensive renovation has just been completed, and the palatial hotel glows throughout its ten stories with all its original elegance. (It has been given a Mobil four-star rating since 1978.)

The Don Ce Sar is at the southern end of the island of St. Petersburg Beach directly on the Gulf of Mexico. You can't miss it. It's the only thing around that is both huge and pink. The Don Ce Sar, A Registry Resort, 3400 Gulf Boulevard, St. Petersburg, FL 33706; (813) 360–1881.

Directly south of St. Petersburg Beach is sprawling **Fort DeSoto Park,** a great place to get away from it all and spend some quiet time with the pelicans and great white herons. Its 900 acres, with more than seven miles of waterfront and almost three miles of fine swimming beaches, ramble over

The Don Ce Sar

five islands: Madeline Key, St. Jean Key, St. Christopher Key, Bonne Fortune Key and the main island–Mullet Key.

Ponce de Leon anchored off Mullet Key during the summer of 1513 to clean the barnacles off the bottom of his ship. He was interrupted by Indians who thought he had no business in their territory. In the skirmish that followed, the first white soldier known to be killed in North America died. Apparently, Ponce de Leon didn't get the message that he was not welcome in the area. When he returned in 1521, he again fought with the Indians, this time receiving the wound that later caused his death in Havana, Cuba.

Construction of Fort DeSoto began in 1898 and was completed two years later. Its eight 12-inch mortars never fired a single shot at any enemy. The remains of this old fort graphically illustrated the then popular concept of harbor defense. Today, it is an interesting relic of history, a good place to climb for a view of the surrounding sea.

Two islands provide a haven for campers, ancient oaks on the northern end of Mullet Key shade a lovely picnicking area, and lifeguards are on duty at the swimming beaches. There is a boat launching ramp, two fishing piers and a small restaurant and gift shop near the fort.

By car, you can get to Fort DeSoto Park only by a toll bridge from the north. To leave, you retrace your path over the toll bridge. This county park wants you to know, however, that the money goes to the State Road Department and not to the park; (813) 462–3347.

Off the Beaten Path in Southwest Florida

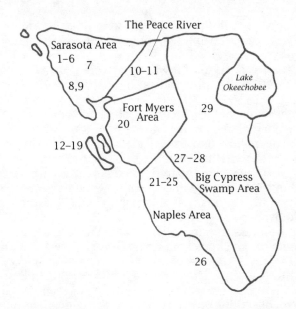

The Peace River

Sarasota Area
1–6
7

8,9

10–11

Lake
Okeechobee

Fort Myers
Area
20

29

12–19

27–28

21–25

Big Cypress
Swamp Area

Naples Area

26

Southwest Florida

Sarasota Area

Aficionados of the arts feel right at home in Sarasota, which offers the appealing combination of sandy beaches and sophistication. Settled in 1842, the city's attributes were not really appreciated until it was "discovered" by a Chicago socialite in 1910. Wealthy and influential northerners followed, and in 1927 John Ringling decided this would be the ideal winter quarters for his circus. John and Mable Ringling were instrumental in making Sarasota what it is today.

"The Greatest Show on Earth" made a fortune for Ringling, who knew just what he wanted to do with his money. He built his dream mansion, poured millions into his art collections and invested heavily in civic improvements for Sarasota. The Ringling enthusiasm was contagious, and the city became known as a mecca for the arts.

Today's proliferating art galleries and theatres are direct descendants of the circus king's munificence. The **John and Mable Ringling Museum of Art** gives visitors a chance to see a cultural complex that puts Florida on the fine arts map. Included are a museum of art with one of the most distinguished collections of Baroque art in the hemisphere, the **Asolo Theatre** (an eighteenth-century theatre imported in its entirety from Asolo, Italy), a **museum of the circus** and **John Ringling's home.**

To call Ca'd'Zan (meaning house of John) simply Ringling's home doesn't quite do it justice. The thirty-two—room mansion on Sarasota Bay, patterned after the Doge's Palace on the Grand Canal in Venice, is one of America's great historic houses. Built in the 1920s at a cost of more than $1,500,000, this stately residence features a huge crystal chandelier from the lobby of New York's Waldorf Astoria Hotel and is elaborately furnished with art objects from around the world.

While officially it was known as the house of John, Mable Ringling had a lot to say about the design. She insisted on including the tower of the old Madison Square Garden (where the circus regularly appeared) in the plans. The architects had some problems with the tower in combination with the Venetian Palace idea, but gave in when Mable declared, "It is my house. I know what I want and that is that."

The Ringling Complex is open daily 10:00 A.M.—6:00 P.M., Thursday 10:00 A.M.—10:00 P.M. According to a stipulation in John Ringling's will, the museum's art galleries are open without charge to everyone on Saturday. A pleasant snack pavilion is located near the Circus Museum. The complex is located on U.S. 41, 3 miles north of downtown Sarasota. The John and Mable Ringling Museum of Art, The State Art Museum of Florida, 5401 Bay Shore Road, Sarasota, FL 34243; (813) 355–5101.

Did you know that at least twenty-seven species of sharks inhabit the Gulf of Mexico off Sarasota? Were you aware that over 600 species of fish and even more invertebrates live in Sarasota's Gulf and Bay waters? If you'd like to know more about these creatures of the deep, stop in at the **Mote Marine Science Center.** Guides will introduce you to the residents of thirty-six aquaria including "Nibbles" the Nurse Shark. The sea horses and sea turtles are especially popular, as is the extensive shell collection. The Research Exhibits provide the inside scoop on current scientific projects and explain how this research applies to our lives. From downtown Sarasota, follow Co. Rd. 780 to St. Armands Circle, continue to New Pass Bridge Area, look for directional signs. Open 10:00 A.M.—5:00 P.M. daily. Mote Marine Science Center, 1600 City Island Park, Sarasota, FL 33577; (813) 388–2451.

Orchid lovers should spend some time browsing the extensive collection of tropical plants at the **Marie Selby Botanical Gardens.** This garden focuses on epiphytes—orchids, bromeliads, gesneriads and aroids. The research done here is vitally important because the tropical forests and jungles of the world are fast disappearing and with them are going many rare and beautiful plants. The Eric Young Micropropagation Centre is a modern tissue culture laboratory dedicated to the research of cloning rare plants.

You'll enjoy strolling through the waterfront gardens and seeing the greenhouse abloom with elegant air plants. The gift and book shop has tropical plants for sale along with books on everything you ever wanted to know about gardening. The gardens are located at U.S. 41 and South Palm

Avenue, 4¹/₂ miles south of the Sarasota—Bradenton Airport. Open 10:00 A.M.—5:00 P.M. every day of the year. The Marie Selby Botanical Gardens, 811 S. Palm Avenue, Sarasota, Florida. If you wish to have a guided tour, be sure to call ahead: (813) 366–5730.

Myakka River State Park—28,000 acres of river, lakes, marsh, hammocks and prairies—is one of the country's outstanding wildlife sanctuaries and breeding grounds. A five-mile drive through this scenic park will acquaint you with the overall features of the area, but to really experience its

Gator Gal **at Myakka River State Park**

incredible diversity, why not rent a bike or, better yet, a canoe. Camping opportunities range from rustic cabins to a backpack trail that leads to four primitive camping areas.

Bird-watchers will feel that their time on the lakeshore birdwalk and observation platform has been well spent when they catch sight of a majestic bald eagle, great blue heron, sandhill crane, egret or ibis.

Some 200 species of birds have been spotted in the park, and there are large rookeries. Board *Gator Gal,* the world's largest air boat (closed during September), or the special Safari Tram (open December through May) for a scenic cruise. Both excursions are narrated by knowledgeable guides. The park is 14 miles east of Sarasota on SR 72. Open daily 8:00 A.M.—sunset; (813) 924–1027.

Basket lovers beware! **Basketville** boasts the largest selection of baskets in the world, a claim you're sure to believe when you try to make up your mind to purchase something. You'll be swamped with choices that range from handcrafted baskets of white ash and red oak to a tremendous variety of permanent flowers, buckets, wooden ware, wicker furniture accessories and handmade imports from all over the world. Basketville is on U.S. 41 four miles south of Venice (4011 S. Tamiami Trail). Open daily 8:00 A.M.—6:00 P.M.; (813) 493–0007.

Because they are near the longest sloping continental shelf in the world, the **beaches around Venice** are a fertile fossil hunting area, especially for shark teeth. Some of the teeth being washed ashore belong to creatures that have been extinct for millions of years. Put on your swimsuit and start scooping up sand in the shallow water. Keep a sharp eye out. Some teeth are very tiny. Free.

The Peace River

More shark teeth, some as large as your hand, can be found in the **Peace River.** In fact, a canoe trip down the pristine Peace can provide you with one of your very best off-the-beaten-track experiences in the entire state. Florida's most uninhabited waterway winds its tranquil way (too shallow for motor boats) from a source in central Florida's Green

83

Swamp to the Gulf of Mexico. Once the Peace marked the boundary between Indian territory to the east and white settler's land to the west.

Every bend in the river is a movie set of palmettos, pine, cypress knees and long strands of gray Spanish moss hanging from the gnarled limbs of live oaks. Wild flowers line the banks and large water birds stand in the shallows. You may spot armadillos, alligators and deer. You will surely see cows that belong to the cattle ranches you paddle through. The perfectly clear water makes fossil finding easy, and there are many lovely spots to camp along the river banks.

Tailor your trip length to your own whims. Half-day trips are fun, but, to really get in tune with this beautiful river, plan to spend several days. Put your canoe in at the bridge in Bartow, Ft. Meade, Bowling Green, Wauchula, Zolfo Springs, Gardner, Brownsville, Arcadia or Nocatee.

The friendly folks at **Canoe Outpost** will help select the right trip for you, answer all your questions and provide whatever you need to be comfortable and safe. They can furnish either transportation upstream or pick-up downstream, canoes, paddles, life cushions, all camping gear, coolers and ice. Open year-round. Canoe Outpost (a mile northwest of Arcadia on Co. Rd. 661), Rte. 7, Box 301, Arcadia, FL 33821; (813) 494–1215.

Fort Myers Area

It's hard to resist such a huge collection of shells and coral. Pick out your own oyster (complete with pearl), examine rare shells from the seven seas, or select just the right piece of precious black coral. The **Shell Factory** has over 70,000 square feet of temptations, which include gourmet food, imported gifts, beachwear and hand-made moccasins. Quite a display! Located on U.S. 41 (N. Tamiami Trail) 4 miles north of Fort Myers. Open seven days a week 9:30 A.M.—6:00 P.M.; (813) 995–2141.

Sanibel Island's fortunate location enables it to snare some of the ocean's most beautiful treasures. This pretty island has a well-deserved reputation as one of the three best shelling beaches on earth. (The others are in Africa and the Southwest Pacific.) Beachcombers take their hobby very seriously, pacing the shoreline with bodies bent in a position known locally as the "Sanibel Stoop."

Nearly half of the land on Sanibel and the adjoining island of Captiva has been preserved in its natural state. The most frequented sanctuary is the J. N. **"Ding" Darling National Wildlife Refuge,** named for a Pulitzer prize—winning political cartoonist. Darling was an ardent conservationist before anyone ever heard the word ecology. This mangrove wilderness at the southern end of the Atlantic flyway is a way station for migrating ducks and shelters more than 200 varieties of birds including the endangered brown pelican. Viewing is best at sunrise or sunset. Visitors can drive, bike or paddle winding canoe trails through the 5,000-acre refuge, which is laced with fishing streams and hiking trails. Visitor's Center open 9:00 A.M.—4:00 P.M. Call (813) 472–1100.

Useppa Island has a beach that looks like it was yanked from the South Pacific, a swimming pool, tennis court, three-hole golf course and deepwater marina. Best of all, it has a profusion of lush tropical vegetation—palms, royal poinciana and massive banyans.

Useppa is considered the most beautiful island in the chain of islands in Pine Island Sound, but its air of serenity hides a tempestuous past. The Calusa Indians apparently found it appealing. Archaeologists claim this is the oldest continuously occupied land mass on the western Florida coast. (The Indians started piling up oyster shell mounds in 3500 B.C.)

For a while the notorious pirate, Jose Gaspar, held his favorite female captive here. (The run-of-the-mill ladies were kept in a group on the nearby island named for these unsavory goings on—Isle de las Captivas, now known as Captiva Island.) Joseffa was a headstrong sixteen-year-old who never did take to Gaspar. He found this so withering to his ego that he chopped off her head. As you can imagine, this place has its share of ghost stories. (Local dialect changed Joseffa to Useppa.)

Streetcar tycoon John Roach bought Useppa in 1894, and publisher Barron Collier purchased it in 1912. Lots of rich and famous folks liked the combination of beauty and privacy that this tiny half-mile-long island afforded. Theodore Roosevelt, the Vanderbilts, the Rockefellers, Zane Grey and

85

Mae West stopped in from time to time, and the Izaak Walton Fishing Club was founded here. More recently, Useppa served as the training ground for the Bay of Pigs invasion.

Neglect and deterioration threatened to scuttle the island's charm, but Gar Beckstead arrived just in time. In 1976 he purchased Useppa, moved his family there and started the long process of restoration. In his mission to recapture the past, Gar uncovered one historic treasure after another, including a bathtub full of signed tarpon scales. To stroll the east ridge's pink pathway to the old Collier Inn is to return to the era of the 1920s. Architecture is strictly controlled and new cottages are all white frame with lattice work and wide screened porches to match their restored counterparts. No cars intrude on the quiet.

Today the island is run as a private club, but nonmembers are welcome to stay as long as a week on an "investigatory" visit. (Members arrive by boat or seaplane.) A wide range of rental accommodations are available.

If you prefer a day trip, sign up with South Seas Plantation on Captiva Island. (Useppa is approximately 9 miles north of Captiva.) *The Silver Lady,* a 150-passenger, double-decked excursion boat, takes passengers through scenic Pine Island Sound while the captain points out leaping dolphins and baby ospreys peering from nests on the channel markers. Luncheon and dinner cruises allow time to explore as well as to savor a leisurely repast in Collier Inn. (For reservations at South Seas Plantation or information about the trip to Useppa, call (813) 472–5111, extension 3329.)

If your yacht is less than 100 feet, the marina can accommodate it. Useppa Island lies just 2 miles south of Boca Grande Pass at Marker 63 on the Intracoastal Waterway, midway between Naples and Sarasota on the southwest coast of Florida. Useppa Island Club, P. O. Box 640, Bokwelie, FL 33922; (813) 283–1061.

Cabbage Key was once home of playwright and mystery novelist Mary Roberts Reinhart. Her house, built in 1938 on the highest point of the island, has been converted into Cabbage Key Hide-Away Inn and Restaurant. One memorable feature of the inn is its "wall paper" worth more than $22,000. Somewhere along the way, the guests started tacking one dollar bills to the walls and signing them. Today, these bills cover the ceilings, walls and beams. Visitors get a kick out of locating "their" dollar when returning to Cabbage Key.

Cabbage Key is a popular watering hole with excellent docking facilities. You might want to explore the nature trails before dining on one of the outdoor porches. (Don't forget your insect repellent.) Accessible only by boat or seaplane, Cabbage Key is at Channel Marker 60 in the Intracoastal Waterway. Lunch and dinner cruises run regularly from Captiva's South Seas Plantation. (For information, call (813) 472–5111.) Cabbage Key is 5 miles south of Charlotte Harbour on Intracoastal Waterway near marker 60. To reach the inn, call (813) 283–2278.

Another way to get to these idyllic islands is by signing on with an **Adventure Sailing Escape flotilla.** Each afternoon finds the flotilla docked at a resort on a different island. You'll have full guest privileges including pools, golf courses, tennis courts, game rooms, entertainment and dancing in most resorts and hot showers, laundries and shopping at all of them. Meals are taken in the resorts' casual dining rooms with breakfasts serving as chart sessions for that day's trip. The possibilities during a week's flotilla are South Seas Plantation, 'Tween-Waters Inn, Burnt Store Marina, Useppa Island Club, Cabbage Key Hide-Away, Miller's Marina, Sonesta Sanibel Harbor and Island Harbour Resort.

To guarantee that anyone may participate, a two-day skipper school precedes each flotilla departure. Novices and those without large boat experience sign up for instruction on docking under power, basic sailing, chart reading and radio operation. Qualified sailors may skip this part. Once the flotilla departs, there is no onboard supervision. Everyone skippers and everyone crews. There are sixteen yachts to choose from and they range from 27 to 41 feet with from two to eight berths. No more than five boats sail in any flotilla. Royal Palm Tours, Inc., P.O. Box 06079, Fort Myers, FL 33907; (813) 489–0344.

Fort Myers got its start as a military post during the Seminole Indian wars. Abandoned after a brief occupation by federal troops during the Civil War, the fort became the center of a tiny village reached, in those days, by boat. Majestic palm-lined avenues and a profusion of exotic flowers and fruit trees contribute to Fort Myer's tropical good looks.

Thomas Edison, who made his winter home here, imported 200 royal palms from Cuba in 1900, starting Fort Myers on its way to being known as a "City of Palms." Edison was a great promoter of Fort Myers and wanted to bestow the fruits of his genius on the local citizenry. Soon after perfecting the electric lamp, he offered to provide the entire city with electric streetlights. The town voted against the proposal when many expressed fear that the lights would keep the cows from getting a good night's sleep.

Thomas Edison's winter residence, complete with chandeliers still burning with their original carbon filament bulbs, is open to the public. Edison held 1,096 patents and many of his inventions are on display in the adjoining museum. You cannot help being impressed and inspired by this inventor's philosophy and achievements. Unusual plants and trees from the far corners of the globe flourish on his 14-acre homesite on the Caloosahatchee River. Open 9:00 A.M.—4:00 P.M., Monday through Sunday, 12:30—4:00 P.M. on Sunday. 2350 McGregor Boulevard, Fort Myers, FL 33901; (813) 334–3614.

Those who want to talk to the manatees should head for the **Florida Power and Light Park** on SR 80 east of Fort Myers. The best viewing times are cold mornings when these endangered "sea cows" are toasting their flippers in the warm waters of the power plant discharge. You may park your car alongside the lagoon south of SR 80. Open daily during daylight hours. Free.

The world is not flat, but round. Columbus proved it and you're sure, right? But can you really be sure that the earth isn't hollow, that life doesn't cover its inner walls and that the sun isn't actually in the center of this round sphere? If you find these thoughts intriguing, you should stop in at the **Koreshan State Historic Site.**

Dr. Teed, a physician from Chicago, founded a utopian commune here in the later 1800s. The doctor brought a group with him from Chicago, but the movement never caught on, though some of his followers still publish a newspaper and magazine. For one thing, there were no children to carry the banner for Dr. Teed because he insisted everyone practice celibacy. You may visit the tropical garden and restored village of this pioneer settlement and learn how Dr. Teed went about proving his theories in the museum. This is also a good place to camp and canoe. Open daily 8:00 A.M. to sunset. Guided tours given according to seasonal demand. Take Interstate 75, exit 19. Off U. S. 41, Estero, FL 33928; (813) 992–0311.

Naples Area

The city of Naples caters to the upper crust with all the amenities money can buy, but it has not forgotten the less-well-heeled folk who have the run of its splendid seven-mile public beach and **1,000-foot fishing pier.** Shoppers will look a long time before finding such a marvelous assortment of shops. If your credit cards are suffering from lack of use, don't worry. Shopping in Naples is guaranteed to get them back in the swing of things.

Browsers are more than welcome at the **Old Marine Market Place,** better known as Tin City. A carefully preserved part of Naples's past, now restored, awaits right on Naples Bay at 1200 Fifth Avenue S. This old-fashioned shopping bazaar was created from historic boat buildings connected by cobbled and planked river walks and comes complete with waterfront dining and open air markets. (The Tin City Queen Riverboat offers daily cruises from the marina.) Don't miss the chic stores on Third Street and those marvelously posh emporiums on Fifth Avenue.

Longtime Naples resident Michael Watkins, general manager of the landmark Naples Beach Hotel and Golf Club, contends the best way to see this attractive area is by bike. His suggested route includes stops at Lowdermilk Park, the Conservancy Nature Center, Tin City, the restored historic Naples Depot, Cambier Park, Naples Fishing Pier and the shops on Fifth Avenue and Third Street. In the process, you'll pass through some gorgeous residential real estate. Bikes are available for rent at the hotel's front desk, along with complimentary bicycle maps. For information or reservations, contact The **Naples Beach Hotel and Golf Club,** 851 Gulf Shore Boulevard N., Naples, FL 33940; (813) 261–2222.

The **Conservancy Nature Center** is, surprisingly, on a wooded 14-acre site right in the middle of Naples. The

Natural Science Museum contains natural history, animal and marine displays and participatory exhibits including a computer game, shell game, weather station and marine life touch-tank. Be sure to stroll the two nature trails and visit the recuperating animals and birds (mostly eagles, hawks and owls) in the Animal Rehabilitation Clinic. Tours of this center are given to the public Monday through Thursday 9:30 A.M.—noon and 1:00—4:30 in the afternoon. Half-hour powerboat trips run from December through March.

This private, non-profit organization is dedicated to environmental protection, conservation, wildlife rehabilitation, nature education and ecological research. The Conservancy Nature Center, 1450 Merrihue Drive, Naples, FL 33942 (one block east of Goodlette Road). Open Monday through Saturday from October to May and Monday through Friday June through September. Open daily January, February and March (Sunday 1:00—5:00 P.M.). Nature Center grounds open 8:30 A.M.—5:00 P.M., closed Sunday; (813) 262-0304. Free.

For casual waterfront dining (on outdoor picnic tables, if you wish), you should seek out the **Lighthouse Restaurant.** While peeling your shrimp and sipping a cold beer, you can watch the waterskiers zip by and the sea gulls hover. (Please, heed the sign which asks you NOT to feed the birds. There's a very good reason for it.) The atmosphere is relaxed, the service friendly and the jumbo sandwiches excellent. Open Sunday noon—10:00 P.M., all other days 11:00 A.M.—11:00 P.M. Lighthouse Restaurant, 9180 Gulf Shore Drive N., Naples, FL 33963; (813) 597-2551. Inexpensive to moderate.

Thirty miles to the south of Naples are the **Ten Thousand Islands.** This maze of mangrove islands teeming with fish and bird life is best approached with a guide. Conducted tours leave from Everglades City, the entrance to the western portion of Everglades National Park. This is literally the jumping off place, because access to the wilderness is by water.

One of the most satisfying ways to explore these islands, if insect repellent is at hand, is by canoe. To glide quietly by an egret rookery, to listen to the beat of many wings as flocks pass overhead and to watch the evening sun beam a path of orange across a silent sea is to know Florida at its very best.

Sightseeing tours into the Ten Thousand Islands region and the mangrove swamps of the northwestern Everglades leave from the Gulf Coast Ranger Station between November 1 and May 1. For information about boat tours (available year-round) and boat rentals at the Gulf Coast Ranger Station, write the concessioner at Everglades National Park Boat Tours, P. O. Box 119, Everglades City, FL 33929, or call Everglades National Park: (305) 247–6211.

Big Cypress Swamp Area

Corkscrew Swamp Wildlife Sanctuary, maintained by the National Audubon Society, is a 6,000-acre preserve with a dwindling population of wood storks. These rare large birds, dangerously close to extinction, are definitely worth the trip. The most interesting time to visit is from December through March when the storks nest and breed. Their breeding is timed so that young storks are raised when food is plentiful (which depends entirely on receding water levels to concentrate the fish). An unexpected rainstorm at the wrong time of year can mess up the whole process. (A single family of wood storks requires 440 pounds of food per breeding season!) The frantic activity of the nesting season is something to see. The male gathers the sticks for the nest, the female arranges them and young storks kick up quite a racket.

The sanctuary also protects the largest stand of virgin bald cypress trees in the country. A boardwalk trail (1$\frac{3}{4}$ miles long) winds through this primeval forest of huge trees, some more than 700 years old! An illustrated self-guiding tour booklet describes plants and animals, and there are members of the staff along the way to answer questions. You'll see lots of birds, turtles and alligators along with a variety of lush plant life.

Take a lunch to eat in the pleasant picnic area, because there isn't anyplace nearby to buy so much as a snack. The sanctuary is located 21 miles east of Bonita Springs, 14 miles from Immokalee and 21 miles from U.S. 41. The entrance on Co. Rd. 849 is 1$\frac{1}{2}$ miles from Co. Rd. 846. No pets admitted and overnight camping is not permitted within sanctuary boundaries or in parking area. The Visitor Center and board-walk are open daily 9:00 A.M.—5:00 P.M. For information write: Chief Naturalist, Corkscrew Swamp Sanctuary, Rte. 6, Box 1875-A, Naples, FL 33964, or call (813) 657–3771.

Corkscrew Swamp Sanctuary is at the northern end of **Big Cypress Swamp,** a vast wilderness area administered by the National Park Service. You may explore the swamp by car on Alligator Alley (SR 84) and Tamiami Trail (U.S. 41), which are connected by SR 29 and graded dirt Turner River Road (Co. Rd. 839). The fascinating Loop Road (Co. Rd. 94) from 40-Mile Bend to Monroe Station is only paved for eight miles. Be careful on unpaved roads as they can be dusty and rough or, worse, muddy, as in stuck-in-the-mud.

Approximately one-third of Big Cypress is covered by cypress and the rest is given over to prairies of saw grass, mixed hardwood hammocks, marshes and estuarine mangrove forests. You may also see alligator, wild turkey, deer, mink, bald eagle, ibis, heron, egret and wood stork. The National Park Service has visitor information centers at Preserve Headquarters and at the Oasis Ranger Station. Preserve Headquarters are on Satinwood Drive, Star Route Box 110, west of Ochopee, Florida. The Oasis Ranger Station is 55 miles east of Naples on U. S. 41 in the Preserve. For information write: Park Superintendent, Big Cypress National Preserve, Star Route Box 110, Ochopee, FL 33943, or call (813) 695–4111 or 263–3532.

If your wanderings take you to Sunniland on SR 29, you should know about the Sunniland Cafe. Your first clue will be a sign reading: "Sunniland Cafe—Terrible Food—Worse Service—Far Out Place—For—Far Out People—Welcome." Well, there are worse greetings in the midst of a swamp than welcome. There are also worse signs: "Welcome to Beautiful Downtown Sunniland. Home of the Famous Sunniland Country Club. Eat Here and Get Gas and Worms." Or "For Sale—1983 Henway." Don't ask, "What's a Henway?" The answer is about five pounds. Sunniland Cafe's owner insists you've got to do something to attract folks "out here in the swamp." If you're wearing shoes and a shirt, you can breakfast or lunch with the local crowd. A comforting sign announces: "Same Day Service On Most Orders." Good luck. Inexpensive.

Those continuing north on SR 29 will eventually come to Palmdale and the **Cypress Knee Museum.** Tom Gaskins experiments in controlled cypress knee growth, and some of his creations are not to be believed. You'll be fascinated by the museum, which is built around the world's largest transplanted cypress tree. At the factory you may watch cypress knees being peeled and perhaps pick up a souvenir in the sales room. Save the best for last—a 3/4-mile catwalk stroll through a cypress swamp, cabbage palm and oak hammock and bayhead.

The sign in front of the museum assures visitors that it was built by a "selfish reactionary" without any help from "city, county, state or federal government" and that it contains "souvenirs of a time before civilization covered the United States." Should you need further encouragement, the signs on U.S. 27 have a particular urgency to them: "Lady, If He Won't Stop, Hit Him On The Head With A Shoe." Cypress Knee Museum is 1 mile south of Palmdale, near the junction of U.S. 27 and SR 29. Open daily 8:00 A.M. to sundown. If you're under age twelve or over age eighty, you get in free. (813) 675–2951.

Off the Beaten Path in Southeast Florida

1. Elliott Museum
2. Gilbert's Bar House of Refuge
3. Lake Okeechobee
4. Jonathan Dickinson State Park
5. Jupiter Lighthouse
6. Henry Morrison Flagler Museum
7. Norton Gallery of Art
8. Morikami Park, Museum and Gardens
9. Cap's Place
10. Pompano Beach Historical Museum
11. *Jungle Queen*
12. Stranahan House
13. Discovery Center
14. Museum of Art
15. Flamingo Gardens
16. Davie Rodeo Arena
17. Cloisters of the Monastery of St. Bernard de Clairvaux
18. Miami Beach Historic Architectural District
19. Bill Baggs Cape Florida State Recreation Area
20. Little Havana
21. Vizcaya Museum and Gardens
22. The Barnacle
23. Parrot Jungle
24. Monkey Jungle
25. Fruit and Spice Park
26. Cauley Square Village Shops and Tea Room
27. Everglades National Park
28. Sightseeing boats
29. Shark Valley
30. Miccosukee Indian Village

Southeast Florida

Atlantic Coast

Sebastian Inlet State Recreation Area is now an ocean playground, but you would have a hard time telling that to the survivors of the fleet of ships that went down here in 1715. Spanish galleons, loaded with gold and silver, were pummeled by a terrible storm before they sank to the bottom of the sea. At the McLarty Visitor Center you'll see artifacts of the Ais Indians, as well as exhibits and dioramas on the Spanish treasure. The salvage efforts, both historic and recent, are a story in themselves.

Located in Sebastian Inlet on SR A1A about midway between Melbourne and Vero Beach, the area offers outstanding fishing and camping. The time to beachcomb for ancient pieces of eight is right after a storm. You'll need a lot of luck, but it's not impossible. Sebastian Inlet State Recreation Area, 9700 South A1A, Melbourne, FL 32951; (407) 984–4852. The center is open Wednesday through Sunday during the winter 10:00 A.M.—5:00 P.M. and Saturday and Sunday 10:00 A.M.—5:00 P.M. during the summer.

How can you resist a look at the Driftwood Inn in Vero Beach, especially when you hear how this rickety looking "Menagerie of Monstrosities" got started? Some residents remember Waldo Sexton creating his architectural extravaganza from driftwood in the 1930s. He would pace up and down the beach shouting instructions to crews who were working without plans. As a result, nothing seems to be square or level, but does this place ever have character!

Sexton filled his inn with a conglomeration of objects ranging from ships' wheels to early Italian chests and a vast collection of bells. Sexton used to love to show off his collection to visitors and regale them with tales of how he acquired each piece. When one woman took the tour two days in a row, she was amazed to discover these delightful stories had totally changed from one day to the next. When she pointed out the discrepancy to Waldo, he replied, "Madame, I'd rather be a liar than a bore any day."

Lunch at Waldo's, among the antiques, is fun. On a nice day you can eat by the pool overlooking the ocean. A menu that announces, "We'll a la mode anything" can't really miss. You might start off with a cup of Key West Conch Chowder or some conch fritters (the recipe came from a Calusa Indian). Waldo's own nacho burger smothered with nachos, chili, cheese and onions is a delicious challenge. Top it off with Boston's Charles River Pie (coffee ice cream in a cookie crust). (407) 231–7091. The Driftwood Inn Resort is at 3150 S. Ocean Drive, Vero Beach, FL 32960; (407) 231–0550. Lunches are inexpensive.

The **Elliott Museum** is really more like a tiny town. Besides a dozen Early American shops brought from Salem, Massachusetts, there are antique automobiles, motorcycles, Seminole artifacts, a shell collection and a contemporary art gallery. The museum was built in 1961 by Sterling Elliott's son to house his father's inventions, which included the first addressing machine, a knot-tying machine and the original quadracycle. On Hutchinson Island's Ocean Boulevard near Stuart. Open daily 1:00—4:00 P.M.; (407) 225–1961.

The **Gilbert's Bar House of Refuge** (1875) is the last of eleven original structures built along the coast in the 1800s to rescue shipwrecked sailors. This National Historic Site perched on a rocky cliff contains a sea aquarium and a boathouse with early lifesaving equipment. The House of Refuge is on Hutchinson Island near Stuart. Follow signs that take you through Indian River Plantation. The entrance is south of the plantation. Open daily except Monday 1:00—4:15 P.M.; (407) 225–1875.

If you'd like to view water traffic negotiating the 14-foot St. Lucie Locks, drive 8 miles southwest of Stuart on SR 76 for a look.

Bass fishermen should head for **Lake Okeechobee,** about 40 miles inland, which is the second largest lake wholly within the United States. It might encourage you to know more than 3,500,000 pounds of fish (including both sport and commercial catches) are caught here every year. Take your pick of fishing camps; they are all over the place. A fine place to view this impressive body of water is from the Pahokee Observation Tower on top of Hoover Dike in the Pahokee Marina and Campground 10 miles north of Belle Glade. The area is in Pahokee off U.S. 441. Call (407) 924–7832.

Back on the coast, Blowing Rock Preserve on Jupiter Island is worth a ten-minute walk through a pine forest. When a stiff wind is coming out of the northeast, the surf surges through holes in the rocks to create spectacular geysers.

It's only 85 feet high, but in Florida they call it a mountain even if it is only an overgrown sand dune. Add a 25-foot observation tower to Hobe Mountain in **Jonathan Dickinson State Park** and you have a good view of ocean and the surrounding woodlands.

The park was named for a Quaker who was shipwrecked nearby in 1696, discovered by Indians and survived all sorts of traumas before getting his wife and baby safely home to Philadelphia. His journal provides valuable insight into early Florida.

An exciting way to see the park is a trip down the Loxahatchee River to Trapper Nelson's camp. The Loxahatchee is the only National Wild and Scenic River in the state of Florida, and you really ought to experience it. Take the thirty-passenger pontoon boat, *Loxahatchee Queen,* or rent a canoe and paddle past the alligators and bald eagles to Trapper Nelson's. The boat ride takes almost two hours; if you paddle yourself, count on three hours. Alas, the legendary Trapper Nelson is no longer with us, but a ranger will fill you in on some of his eccentricities.

A wide range of activities includes fishing (both salt- and freshwater), boating, camping, and bicycling. The park, on U. S. 1 six miles north of Jupiter, is open 8:00 A.M. to sunset year-round but if you're interested in the boat trip, call because it does not go every day. Jonathan Dickinson State Park, 16450 S. E. Federal Highway, Hobe Sound, FL 33455; (407) 546–2771.

In Jupiter, the 105-foot red brick **Jupiter Lighthouse** is one of the oldest (1860) lighthouses on the Atlantic coast. Still functioning and operated by the Coast Guard as a navigational aid, its current duties include tracking satellites. The Lighthouse, beside Jupiter Inlet, provides a fine view of the Gulf Stream, but its museum is only open noon—2:30 P.M. on Sundays. Jupiter; (407) 746–3181. Free.

A great place to contemplate the Jupiter Lighthouse and watch a steady stream of boats passing at the same time is

Harpoon Louie's. You may eat inside or, better yet, on the expansive deck. Start the day with sundance eggs (in baked potato skins) or Irish country porridge. Louie puts together a memorable peanut butter and jelly sandwich, and his hot dog steamed in beer is not bad either. For dinner you can't do better than fresh fish char-grilled on open coals with a liberal dose of garlic butter sauce. The restaurant is open 7:00 A.M.—10:00 P.M. seven days a week. Easy to find, it's right across from the Jupiter Lighthouse. Prices range from inexpensive to moderate, Jupiter; (407) 744-1300.

Burt Reynolds is a local boy who put Jupiter on the map while making a name for himself. You may visit his horse ranch, feedstore, western store and petting zoo a short drive from town. A number of movies have been made here.

The western store has a good selection of hats, boots, belts and clothing, as well as a radio station doing business in the right rear corner. If you've been dying for a rattlesnake belt (tongue still intact), this is the place. Photographs of Burt Reynolds starring in numerous films and plays, autographed photos of other stars and Burt's awards adorn the walls.

The feedstore offers dog food in great quantity, and the neatly kept petting zoo has a bunch of friendly animals eagerly awaiting your handful of food. The petting zoo is free. The ranch, open seven days a week 10:00 A.M.—5:00 P.M., is 2 miles down Jupiter Farms Road off Indiantown Road. Look for fancy white wrought iron gates with the initials BR. Call (407) 746-0393.

The Palm Beach area was developing slowly until Henry Flagler pushed his famous railroad south. With the railroad's arrival in 1894 and the grand hotels that Flagler built, Palm Beach quickly established, and still holds, a reputation as an enclave for the ultra wealthy. When Flagler planned his own Palm Beach home, he chose the architectural firm that had built the Metropolitan Opera House and the U. S. Senate Office Building. Described in the press as "more wonderful than any palace in Europe" and costing $4,000,000 in 1901, Whitehall is a showcase that has been marvelously refurbished as the **Henry Morrison Flagler Museum.** The multimillionaire's private railroad car is on display, as are treasures collected from all over the world. The mansion provides a glimpse into the era before income taxes and sets a new standard for the term opulent. The museum is on Whitehall Way, off Coconut Row, in Palm Beach. The Henry Morrison Flagler Museum, P.O. Box 969, Palm Beach, FL 33480. Open Tuesday through Saturday 10:00 A.M.—5:00 P.M., Sunday noon—5:00 P.M.; (407) 655–2833.

The **Norton Gallery of Art** has a reputation as one of the foremost small museums in the United States. Outstanding collections include modern French and American paintings along with some 200 Chinese objects including archaic jades and Buddhist sculpture. The gallery is at 1451 S. Olive Avenue, West Palm Beach, FL 33401. Open Tuesday through Saturday 10:00 A.M.—5:00 P.M., Sunday 1:00—5:00 P.M.; (407) 832–5194. Free.

You may never have heard of George Morikami, but you will be impressed with his life story and the **Morikami Park, Museum and Gardens** he donated. This humble pineapple farmer lived in a modest trailer and never stopped working his fields even though he amassed considerable wealth. You will be asked to remove your shoes (paper slippers provided) before entering the museum where individual rooms are devoted to the tea ceremony, depict a traditional Japanese bedroom or contain photographs of George Morikami and the local Japanese farming community. The tranquil gardens contain bonsai displays. The Morikami Museum of Japanese Culture, 4000 Morikami Park Road, Delray Beach, FL 33446. Open Tuesday through Sunday 10:00 A.M.—5:00 P.M.; (407) 449–0631 or 495–0233.

Did Architect Addison Mizner ever leave his mark on Boca Raton! In 1918 the forty-five—year old, suffering from heart and lung ailments, came to Florida to die. As restless as he was eccentric, he became bored with dying and began designing homes for the super rich. He parlayed his profits into a fortune by wheeling and dealing in real estate and then tackled his real ambition—building a dream city.

He designed The Cloister to be a hotel worthy of being the centerpiece for this splendid project and held a grand opening in February 1926. At the time it was the most expensive 100-room hotel ever built; the style of architecture has been summed up as "Bastard-Spanish-Moorish-Romanesque-Gothic-Renaissance-Bull-Market-Damn-the-Expense." But Florida went quickly from boom to bust and the hotel closed after a single season. Mizner's extravagant vision fizzled, but his pink wedding cake of a hotel was destined to play many roles over the years including one as a World War II barracks.

Today the five-star Boca Raton Hotel and Club, its original splendor intact, thrives in its reincarnation as a premier resort. The hotel is on Camino Real between U. S. 1 and SR A1A and is on the Intracoastal Waterway across from its seaside extension, the Boca Beach Club. Boca Raton Hotel and Club, P. O. Box 225, Boca Raton, FL 33432; (407) 395–3000.

Care to eat where Winston Churchill, Franklin D. Roosevelt and the Vanderbilts once dined? If that list doesn't impress you, how about Casey Stengel and Jack Dempsey? Both notables and nonnotables have been flocking to **Cap's Place** for a long time because of its excellent fresh fish.

Back in the 1920s, this group of wooden shacks attached to an old barge was floated up the Intracoastal Waterway from Miami to its present location on Cap's Island. Once a center for rumrunning and gambling, the restaurant has cleaned up its act, if not its ramshackle appearance, and serves dinner daily from 5:00 P.M.

The trick is knowing how to get there. In Lighthouse Point follow N. E. Twenty-fourth Street toward the ocean. Soon you'll see official looking signs leading the way to Cap's Place. You'll end up in a parking lot. If the boat isn't there, don't worry. It'll arrive soon. After a brief boat ride to the island, a "Welcome to Cap's" sign hoves into view. The building looks pretty run-down, but say hello to the pelicans roosting in the nearby trees and press on.

Inside you'll find a rattlesnake skin on the wall measuring more than six feet and a sign that says "Help preserve wildlife, Throw a party at Cap's." The floors are uneven, but the food is good. You can't miss with a stone crab appetizer (in season), hearts of palm salad, the catch of the day and Key lime pie. Entrees range from moderate to expensive. The boat ride is free, but tips are appreciated on the return trip. Call (407) 941–0418.

You may start longing for the good old days when you learn you used to be able to rent a "Kester" cottage for a month for only $16. Two of these cottages have been restored and furnished with articles that relate to the area's early history. The **Pompano Beach Historical Museum** is at 18 and 20 S. E. Third Avenue (just off the south side of Atlantic Boulevard in Pompano Beach). Open Monday and Wednesday noon—3:00 P.M. and Saturday 1:00—5:00 P.M., closed June through August. (407) 924–0179. Free.

Fort Lauderdale Area

Pompano Beach Air Park is the winter home (November through May) of the *Enterprise,* one of four touring dirigibles in the world. The blimp is 192 feet long, 50 feet wide and 59 feet high. Powered by small engines, it has a cruising speed of 35 mph and can operate eight hours a day for a week on the same amount of fuel it takes to taxi a big jet out to the runway for takeoff. The new Visitor Center, containing exhibits on the history of the blimp, is open to the public. Sorry, you can't take a ride, but you will get a good closeup look at this huge flying machine. 1500 N. E. Fifth Avenue on the west side of Pompano Air Park; (407) 946–8300.

One way to glimpse Fort Lauderdale's glittering waterways is by cruising on the ***Jungle Queen.*** Daily sightseeing cruises at 10:00 A.M. and 2:00 P.M. (dinner cruise at 7:00 P.M.) go up New River and by Millionaires Row with a stop off at Indian Village to see birds, monkeys and real live alligator wrestling. You'll learn something about the history of the area, where the cruise liners in Port Everglades are heading, who lives where and how they made their money. Leaves from Bahia Mar Yacht Basin, 1007 Seabreeze Boulevard, Fort Lauderdale, FL 33316; (407) 462–5596.

Speaking of cruises, thousands of people cruise to exotic ports of call from Port Everglades. More than twenty cruise lines depart from six ultramodern terminals. This is the deepest port between Norfolk and New Orleans and serves more five-star cruise ships than any other port in the nation. You'll get a good view of Port Everglades activity from the S. E. Seventeenth Street Causeway Bridge.

You can watch manatees and tropical fish basking in the warmth of the Port Everglades Power Plant's water discharge from the parking and picnic area on Eisenhower Boulevard and S. E. Twenty-sixth Street.

One of Fort Lauderdale's worst kept secrets is a restaurant

that doesn't advertise and is appropriately named By Word of Mouth. Before you are seated, you are shown all the evening's selections and the host or hostess describes the ingredients and methods of preparation. You may select sun-dried tomato and pesto pâté, a salad of smoked turkey with grated orange, kiwi and jicama, New Mexican cornbread salad, ossobuco, breast of duck with apricot and Grand Marnier and then top the whole thing off with a house favorite, Chocolate Raspberry Cake.

By Word of Mouth is at 3200 N. E. Twelfth Avenue in Fort Lauderdale. The word is out. (Being featured in *Gourmet Magazine* took care of that.) You'd better make a reservation; (305) 564–3663. Expensive.

The **Stranahan House** is a gem. When Frank Stranahan came to take charge of the New River overnight camp in 1893, it was the only outpost on a road between Lake Worth and Lemon City (now North Miami). By the late 1890s, Stranahan's trade with the Seminole Indians was at its peak and winter tourism was in its infancy.

Love and marriage entered Stanahan's life when the first teacher arrived at the new settlement. The couple's restored store/home of classic Florida frontier design is the oldest existing structure in Broward County. The Stranahan House (off Las Olas Boulevard, at the New River tunnel) is at 335 S. E. Sixth Avenue, Fort Lauderdale, FL 33301. Open for tours on Wednesday, Friday and Saturday 10:00 A.M.—4:00 P.M. A Friday night social with beverages, snacks and live music is held 5:30—8:00 P.M. Call (305) 524–4736.

History buffs shouldn't miss the antique-laden King Cromartie House in "Himmarshee Village," the historic preservation area along the New River. You'll find out just how creative those early pioneers had to be. 229 S. W. Second Avenue, Fort Lauderdale, FL 33315. Right next door is the **Discovery Center** (housed in the area's first hotel, the New River Inn) where you may go cave crawling, see bees at work, bend rays of light and touch a star. This hands-on experience in art, science and history is at 231 S. W. Second Avenue, Fort Lauderdale, FL 33301. Open Tuesday through Saturday 10:00 A.M.—5:00 P.M., Sunday 1:00—5:00 P.M.; (305) 462–4115.

Fort Lauderdale's new multimillion dollar **Museum of Art** is a real prize. Some have called its astonishing twentieth-century collection "unsettling" and "disturbing" but none has denied its vitality. The impressive fan-shaped museum features six distinctive exhibition spaces, a sculpture terrace, giftshop, bookstore and art library. It contains the largest collection of ethnographic material in Florida encompassing Oceanic, West African, pre-Columbian and American Indian art.

The museum is at One East Las Olas Boulevard, Fort Lauderdale, FL 33301. Open Tuesday 11:00 A.M.—9:00 P.M., Wednesday through Saturday 10:00 A.M.—5:00 P.M. and Sunday noon—5:00 P.M., closed Monday and all national holidays. Parking is available at the Municipal Parking facility on S. E. First Avenue that borders the museum on the east. Ask for hours of free public tours. Call (305) 525-5500.

The largest tree in Florida, a cluster fig 49 feet in circumference and 108 feet tall, keeps right on growing at **Flamingo Gardens.** That's just the beginning. There are also 60 acres of botanical gardens, an Everglades museum, transportation museum, a tramride, through citrus groves, alligators, monkeys, peacocks and a petting zoo. This is your chance to see a sausage tree, gumbo limbo, fiddlewood and soursop along with other exotic plants and trees. West of Hollywood off SR 84 at 3750 Flamingo Road, Fort Lauderdale, FL 33330. Open 9:00 A.M.—5:00 P.M. daily; (305) 473-0010 or (305) 473-2955.

Everglades Holiday Park is a gateway to the largest subtropical wilderness in the continental United States. One way to get acquainted with the Everglades is by a guided forty-five-minute airboat ride. Tours run continuously 9:00 A.M.—5:00 P.M. daily. You'll see alligators, exotic birds and an endless expanse of sawgrass. The park is at the end of Griffin Road west of U. S. 27, about thirty minutes from Fort Lauderdale and Miami. Call (305) 434-8111.

In Fort Lauderdale when they refer to Davie, Florida, as "out west," they aren't just kidding. Davie is an authentic western town full of real live cowboys and cowgirls. If you'd like to look like they do, stop in at Grifs Western Store, which smells very leathery and sells all manner of boots, hats, shirts, jeans and saddles. Should you arrive by horse, there are hitching posts out front for your convenience. Even the Davie McDonald's sports a corral with salt licks, watering troughs and hitching posts for your steed.

Come Thursday night, folks gather in the new, domed **Davie Rodeo Arena** for some good old-fashioned steer-wrestling, calf-roping and bull riding. This is, by the way, the only weekly jackpot rodeo between Key West and Maine. The rodeo, which begins at 8:00 P.M., is on Griffin Road at Davie Road in Davie, FL 33314; (305) 797–1145.

Miami Area

Where do the Miami Dolphins hole up before a football game? At Miami Lakes Inn and Golf Resort. Take time to stroll the attractive Main Street shopping arcade with its brick walkways, gardens, fountains, movie theatres, sidewalk cafe, restaurants and shops. Seafood lovers should sample the fare at Main Street Restaurant. Open for breakfast, lunch and dinner. Miami Lakes is a twenty-minute drive west of metropolitan Miami and Fort Lauderdale. Just off Rte. 826 N. (Palmetto Expressway). Follow the signs. Miami Lakes Inn and Golf Resort, Main Street, Miami Lakes, FL 33014; (305) 821–1150.

It's amazing what money can do. Publisher William Randolph Hearst wanted a Spanish monastery at his San Simeon castle in California so he bought the **Cloisters of the Monastery of St. Bernard de Clairvaux** and had it shipped from Europe. Only it wasn't quite as simple as it sounds. The monastery arrived in this country in 10,751 crates, but Florida customs officers wouldn't release them because they were worried about hoof-and-mouth bacteria in the packing hay. The monastery was finally reassembled, one piece of stone at a time, after Hearst's death. Built in 1141, this is the oldest building in this hemisphere. You can still see the marks early stonemasons carved in the rock. Open Sunday noon—5:00 P.M.; 10:00 A.M.—5:00 P.M., other days. Located at 16711 W. Dixie Highway in North Miami Beach, FL 33160; (305) 945–1462.

Some of the smaller hotels at the south end of Miami Beach have been getting facelifts, and the heritage of old Miami is being preserved in the process. A square-mile area featuring the distinctive resort atmosphere of the late 1920s and 1930s is being restored. Officially known as the **Miami**

Beach Historic Architectural District (fondly called the "Art Deco District"), this section contains the nation's largest collection of Art Deco structures. The buildings, totalling more than 800, are the first twentieth-century structures to be included on the National Register of Historic Places. The Art Deco District stretches from Sixth to Twenty-third streets between Lenox Court and the ocean in Miami Beach. Tours are available every Saturday beginning at 10:30 A.M. from the Art Deco Welcome Center (which is open every day but Sunday 10:00 A.M.—6:00 P.M.) at 661 Washington Avenue in Miami Beach; (305) 672–2014.

The Sonesta Beach Hotel and Tennis Club on Key Biscayne has a terrific "Just Us Kids" program for children age five to thirteen. Well-trained college students serve as counselors who supervise a wide range of fun (as well as educational) activities. Kids are taken on excursions to Planet Ocean, Metro Zoo, The Science Museum, and Seaquarium. There are also beach and pool activities, contests, games, movies and crafts classes. Kids can participate in any part of each day's activities. The program is offered to hotel guests at no extra charge with the exception of the child's entrance fee to commercial attractions. Sonesta Beach Hotel and Tennis Club, 350 Ocean Drive, Key Biscayne, FL 33149; (305) 361–2021.

Head for the southern end of the island of Key Biscayne for a great view of Biscayne Bay from **Bill Baggs Cape Florida State Recreation Area.** You'll have to climb 122 steps to the top of the lighthouse, but it's well worth it. Just imagine how the keeper and his aide felt in 1836 when Seminole Indians surrounded the lighthouse and tried to burn it down. The trapped men tossed out a keg of gunpowder, which alerted a patrolling ship to the problem and saved the day. The restored keeper's quarters has hand-carved chairs and animal skin seats just as it did in the 1830s. From the beach you get a good view of Stiltsville, a community of fishermen's shacks and homes on stilts looking rather vulnerable out in the bay. Off U. S. 1 at the south end of the island. Guided tours given daily except Tuesday; (305) 361–5811.

A distinctly Latin flavor permeates Miami, but it is most highly concentrated in its Cuban community. The Hispanic heart of the city is found in the colorful section of south-

Cape Florida Lighthouse

western Miami known as **Little Havana.** This cluster of restaurants, nightclubs, cigar factories, fruit stands and shops pulses with the energy of these lively, voluble people. Lingering over an aromatic cup of Cuban coffee and listening to Spanish may make you forget what country you're in. Some recommended restaurants are Malaga, Segovia, Centro Vasco and La Esquina De Tejas. Little Havana is a thirty-block strip on S. W. Eighth Street (known here as Calle Ocho), Miami.

Vizcaya Museum and Gardens is a must-see. Vizcaya is James Deering's Italian Renaissance palace, one of the finest homes ever built in America. Deering, vice president of International Harvester, spent twenty years collecting priceless treasures from around the world before beginning to build a home for them in 1914. After a global search, he selected Biscayne Bay as the ideal location for his winter retreat. The seventy-room palace was finished in 1916 and the formal gardens took five years to complete with as many as a thousand artisans working at a time. The result is a magnificent achievement featuring an extraordinary collection of furnishings and art objects as well as gardens that have been called "the finest in the Western Hemisphere." 3251 S. Miami Avenue, FL 33129. Open daily except Christmas Day 9:30 A.M.—5:00 P.M. Guided tours available. Call (305) 579–2708.

The historic pioneer home known as **The Barnacle** (1891) once belonged to one of Coconut Grove's earliest settlers, Ralph Middleton Munroe. This photographer and naval architect named the tiny village "Coconut Grove" and helped the settlement grow by encouraging his influential northern friends to visit. The resourceful Mr. Munroe first built a one-story building of wood salvaged from shipwrecks. Later, he jacked the house up on stilts and added a new first floor to make room for his growing family. Take note of Munroe's ingenious "air conditioning" system and enjoy the lushly landscaped grounds. Guided tours are Thursday through Monday 9:00 and 10:30 A.M. and 1:00 and 2:30 P.M. Barnacle State Historic Site, 3485 Main Highway, Coconut Grove, FL 33133; (305) 448–9445.

In 1895 early settlers to Coconut Grove built Plymouth Congregational Church, which is considered South Florida's finest example of Spanish Mission architecture. Vines cover the twin belfry towers, a peacock saunters about the grounds, and the church is surrounded by native flora. No wonder this is the most sought after wedding chapel in Miami. It is located at Main Highway and Devon Road. 3429 Devon Road, Coconut Grove, FL 33133; (305) 444–6521.

The amazing thing about Hotel Place St. Michel with its vaulted ceilings, graceful arches, Spanish tiles and antique furnishings is that you don't need a passport to get there. This small European-style inn has mastered the little touches that mean so much to the traveler—a basket of fruit on arrival, a newspaper delivered to your door each morning and a hearty continental breakfast (included in the price of the room) to get you going. (Their warm, flaky croissants are immense!)

Plymouth Congregational Church

The hotel (built in 1926) has been beautifully restored, and each of the thirty rooms has its own distinct personality. Along with all the charm, it's nice to have air conditioning, a phone, color TV and a friendly face at the desk eager to help.

It's also wonderfully convenient to have a relaxing piano bar and elegant French restaurant (Restaurant St. Michel) just an elevator ride away. Breakfast is 7:00—9:30 A.M., lunch 11:30 A.M.—2:30 P.M., dinner 6:00—10:00 P.M. (10:30 P.M. on weekends). Expensive. Sunday brunch is 11:00 A.M.—2:30 P.M.

Hotel Place St. Michel and Restaurant are on the corner of Ponce de Leon Boulevard and Alcazar Avenue. 162 Alcazar Avenue, Coral Gables, FL 33134. Hotel: (305) 444–1666; restaurant: (305) 446–6572.

Parrot Jungle will delight the entire family. This lush setting with brilliantly colored tropical birds flying freely about flowering plants and trees is unique. Parrot Jungle claims to be the only natural, subtropical jungle and gardens in the United States. Besides the abundance of natural beauty, trained parrots and macaws jump rope, play poker, roller-skate and ride bicycles in forty-minute trained bird shows every one and a half hours.

Take time to stroll leisurely along the walkways through the gardens and cactus ravine; it's hard to miss the shocking-pink flamingos at Flamingo Lake. The cafeteria serves both breakfast and lunch. Open daily 8:00 A.M.—5:00 P.M. Eleven miles south of Miami off U. S. 1. Parrot Jungle, 11000 S. W. 57th Avenue, Miami, FL 33156; (305) 666–7834.

Here's a switch. You're in the cage, and the monkeys run free. Hundreds of monkeys, gorillas, baboons and trained chimpanzees swinging freely through a Florida rain forest obviously get a kick out of seeing you confined. Visitors enjoy chimpanzee performances daily in this unusual attraction that boasts the most complete collection of simians in the United States. 9:30 A.M.—5:00 P.M. daily. **Monkey Jungle,** 14805 S. W. 216th Street, Miami, FL 33170; (305) 235–1611.

If it's strange fruit you're after, the **Fruit and Spice Park** probably has it. This 20-acre botanical garden features 200 species and 500 varieties of fruit, nuts and spices from around the world. Self-guided tours include a look at a demonstration herb and vegetable garden. You may want to pick up some exotic fresh, dried, and canned fruits and spices from the park store. The park and store are open daily from 10:00 A.M.—5:00 P.M. Guided tours Saturday and Sunday 1:00—3:00 P.M. year-round plus Wednesday and Friday from early November to late April. North of Homestead at junction of Coconut Palm Drive (248th Street) and Redland Road (S. W. 187th Avenue). Admission and self-guided tours are free. Call (305) 247–5727.

Shoppers have a field day at **Cauley Square Village Shops** in Homestead. The main building of 1920s Spanish-style architecture, constructed by a millionaire tomato farmer, has witnessed some tempestuous times. Stories of loose women and hard drink abound. The scene has changed dramatically, and today you'll find an enchanting clutter of antique clocks, jewelry, gifts, collectibles and pottery.

The little houses that lie in the shadow of the two-story building were hand-built by the pioneers who helped Flagler construct his "Overseas" highway to Key West. The buildings are testimony to the pioneers' ability to survive hurricanes, freezes, floods, epidemics and the Great Depression. New owners have restored these small homes and turned them into cozy boutiques, galleries, crafts booths and a charming garden tearoom. The Horse Emporium, catering to horse lovers, offers to buy, sell, consign and even horse trade. At the Bewitching Woman you'll find exact duplicates of famous perfumes. The Aviary specializes in talking birds, and the Christmas Shoppe offers to deck the halls year-round.

When you've shopped yourself out, take a refreshment break at the **Cauley Square Tea Room.** Hot crabmeat au gratin or an ambrosia salad with finger sandwiches and chased with a glass of bubbly should do the trick. The shops are open Monday through Saturday 10:00 A.M.—4:30 P.M., closed all holidays. The Cauley Square Tea Room phone number is (305) 257–3725. Moderate. Cauley Square is at 22400 Old Dixie Highway, Miami, FL 33170; (305) 258–3543.

Is there such a thing as a strawberryoholic? If you're one (you know who you are), better hunker down beside Burr's Strawberry Farm because you'll never want to leave. Fresh strawberries are the main item here, but there are also tomatoes, pecans, strawberry ice and ice cream sundaes featuring pineapple, mango, coconut and—surprise—strawberry. A strawberry milkshake is a must. Burr's is at 12761 S. W. 216th Street (near Homestead on the road to the Monkey Jungle). Open only during the winter months.

The folks at the Knaus Berry Farm make the best black bottom cake on the entire earth—not to mention outstanding cinnamon rolls, homemade breads (try the dilly bread), herb bread sticks, cookies and, of course, berry pies, berry ice cream and berry jellies. These folks know how to grow a strawberry. One of their recent monsters was too big to fit in a tea cup.

The families who run this vegetable stand/bakery/ice cream stand may look Amish with their long beards, black hats, bonnets and shawls, but they're German Baptists. They believe in peace, brotherhood, temperance and simple living. Because they are baptized by triple immersion, they are sometimes called Dunkers, which comes from the German *tunken* meaning to immerse.

Their stand is open 8:00 A.M.—5:30 P.M. for approximately five months in the winter. Knaus Berry Farm, 15980 S. W. 248th Street, Coconut Palm Drive, Homestead, FL 33031; (305) 247–0668.

The Everglades

There is no place like the Everglades anywhere on the planet. The Indians named it well. They called it *Pa-hay-okee,* which means grassy waters. Much of this unique wilderness consists of a shallow river percolating slowly toward the sea through a vast expanse of grass. Unlike any other river on earth, this one is 50 miles wide and a mere six inches deep. The water drops ever so gradually, only 15 feet over its entire 100-mile course. This is the country's largest remaining subtropical wilderness.

The river of grass seeps southward from Lake Okeechobee to the mangrove-lined rivers along the Gulf Coast through a transition zone where temperate climate blends with subtropic. The many different habitats along the way teem with life. Some plants and animals are tropical species native to the Caribbean Islands. Others are from the temperate zone.

Today the Everglades has generally come to mean all the various environments in the approximately 1¹/₂ million acres encompassed by **Everglades National Park.** Visitors reach the park by taking U.S. 27 to the main park entrance, approximately 10¹/₂ miles southwest of Homestead, Florida. The park road ends at Flamingo on the southern tip of the Florida mainland, a distance of 40 miles from the entrance.

The first thing a visitor will be aware of on the drive from the main entrance are vast prairies of 10-foot-high sedge, which make up the greatest concentration of saw grass in the world. But just as vital to the intricate balance of life are mounded islands called hammocks rising above the river of grass, stands of pine and palmetto and freshwater sloughs.

Labyrinthian mangrove forests, shallow offshore bays and the many dollops of land known as the Ten Thousand Islands also are vital parts of this complex Everglades picture. Ten thousand is really just an approximation because new islands are being formed all the time, some consisting of only a few salt-tolerant mangrove trees. The area has a reputation as a fertile fishing ground, and the bird activity, especially at sunset, is impressive. This watery wilderness is easy to become lost in; it's a good idea to arrange for a guide or join a boat tour in Everglades City.

In the past, few comprehended the true value of the Glades in terms of sheer food production. This natural nursery ground supplies much of the Gulf with shrimp and the entire Eastern seaboard, including New England, with fish. As a spawning ground, it is irreplaceable.

The value of the Everglades reaches far beyond a multimillion dollar fishing industry. Few places anywhere offer greater variety of beautiful, rare and interesting birds. About 300 species have been identified in the park with large water birds—herons, egrets, ibises and spoonbills—getting the greatest share of attention. The sprawling mangrove wilderness, one of the world's most unusual plant communities, is refuge for panther, bobcat, deer, raccoon, diamondback terrapin, alligator, dolphin and manatee as well as a wide variety of fish.

Visitors to the park who expect grand scenery in the tradition of soaring mountains or great canyons will be disappointed. Getting to know the Glades is like any worthwhile relationship. It takes time. The trick to appreciating this wilderness is to be able to absorb its subtleties, and that cannot be done from behind the windows of a car. Trails range from easy walks of less than a half a mile to more strenuous 14-mile hikes. There is as much life per square inch as anywhere else on earth, but this is not the kind of environment that overwhelms. This is a place that whispers.

Park officials recommend that you begin your visit with a stop at the Main Visitor Center near the main park entrance on U. S. 27. There you may view a short film explaining the interrelationships of man and nature in the Everglades, and pick up information that will help you understand the environment and plan your time wisely. Naturalists give hikes, talks, canoe trips, tram tours, demonstrations and campfire programs throughout the year. Activities change daily. One day there may be a sunrise bird walk or a paddle out into Florida Bay or a slough slog cross-country or a moonlight tram tour. Ask at the visitor center for schedules. Other entrances to the park are at Shark Valley on the Tamiami Trail (U.S. 41) and at Everglades City in the northwest corner of the park.

Whether you choose to canoe through the Ten Thousand Islands, cruise the Wilderness Waterway by outboard, take a swamp tromp with a naturalist or explore the various trails on your own, you will be well rewarded. You'll soon discover that the Everglades is as much an experience as it is a place. It is the incomparable pleasure of watching a great blue heron make his dainty-footed way along the shoreline, of coming upon a flock of roseate spoonbills feeding or of listening to a dolphin take a long, deep breath. To see egrets streaming across a sinking orange sun is to glimpse but a sliver of the abundant beauty in this mysterious, ancient land.

For motel or cabin reservations for the Flamingo Lodge write Everglades Park Catering, Flamingo Inn, Flamingo, FL 33030. (The food at Flamingo Lodge, by the way, is very good.) Motel and cabin reservations should be made well in advance by calling (813) 695–3101. Some facilities are closed between June 1 and October 31, so be sure to call ahead.

Park campgrounds, located at Long Pine Key and Flamingo, provide drinking water, picnic tables, grills, tent and

trailer pads and restrooms. Flamingo has cold water showers. Recreation vehicles are permitted, but there are no elec-
trical, water or sewage hookups. Campground stays are lim-
ited to fourteen days from December 1 to March 31. You may
camp, without charge, at other designated sites, on beaches,
or in backcountry. Access is either on foot or by boat. You
must first obtain a free backcountry use permit at the park
entrance station or at a ranger station.

You may explore well-marked canoe trails or chart your
own course. Choose livery service or a complete camping
outfit that meets the special requirements for canoeing in
the Everglades. Glass-bottom boat tours and snorkel trips are
available. Biscayne Aqua Center, 39801 Ingraham Highway,
Homestead, FL 33034; (305) 246–1530.

A well-marked inland water route runs from Flamingo to
Everglades City. Sequentially numbered markers guide you
over its 99 miles. Boats more than 18 feet long or with high
cabins and windshields should not attempt the route
because of narrow channels and overhanging foliage in some
areas. The route requires a minimum of six hours with outboard motor or seven days by canoe. One-day round trips
are not recommended.

Campsites are available along the route. Be sure to notify a
park ranger at either Flamingo or Everglades City both at the
start and the end of your trip. The Flamingo marina, which
can accommodate boats up to 60 feet long, rents small powered skiffs and canoes. Year-round boat tours at Flamingo
travel through the mangrove wilderness and into Florida Bay.

Sightseeing boats go into the Ten Thousand Islands
region and the mangrove swamps of the northwestern Everglades. These concession-operated tours leave from the Gulf
Coast Ranger Station. For information about boat tours and
boat rentals at the Gulf Coast Ranger Station, write the concessioner at Everglades National Park Boat Tours, P. O. Box
119, Everglades City, FL 33929.

Shark Valley lies off U.S. 41, the Tamiami Trail. Here,
along the 15-mile loop road you may see a variety of wildlife
that inhabits the wide shallow waterway, which eventually
empties into Shark River. Alligators, otters, snakes, turtles,
and birds, including rare wood storks and the Everglades
kite, are native to this watery expanse. Hardwood hammocks

and other tree islands dot the landscape. The loop road is used for tram rides, biking and walking. An observation tower along the road provides a spectacular view. Reservations are recommended for seasonal tram rides. For further information contact the Everglades Park Superintendent, Box 279, Homestead, FL 33030; (305) 247–6211.

It's hard to believe the **Miccosukee Indian Village** in the Florida Everglades is just 25 miles west of the gleaming towers of downtown Miami. Approximately 600 contemporary Miccosukees are descendants of some fifty tribespeople who escaped deportation from the United States during the Indian Wars of the last century.

Guided tours include the village of chickee huts where tribal members live in traditional fashion. You may watch Indians wrestle alligators, take an adventurous airboat ride through the Everglades or visit the Indian Museum, which features artifacts from various tribes.

Members of the Miccosukee tribe create and sell handmade dolls, wood carvings, beadwork, basketry, jewelry and other crafts. The restaurant features authentic Miccosukee dishes along with standard American fare. Twenty-five miles west of Miami on U.S. 41 (Tamiami Trail). P. O. Box 440021, Miami, FL 33144. Open daily 9:00 A.M.—5:30 P.M.; (305) 223–8388.

Off the Beaten Path in The Keys

1 — The Keys
2
3
4–7
10
9 — 8
11–22
25,26
23,24 — Key West Area

1. Overseas Highway
2. John Pennekamp
   Coral Reef State Park
3. *African Queen*
4. Theatre of the Sea
5. Indian Key
6. Lignumvitae Key
7. Long Key State Park
8. Seven-mile bridge
9. National Key Deer Refuge
10. Perky Bat Tower
11. Ernest Hemingway
    Home and Museum
12. Sloppy Joe's
13. Audubon House

14. Turtle Kralls
15. Mel Fisher Maritime Heritage
    Society Museum
16. Wrecker's Museum
17. Duval Street
18. Old Island Days
19. Conch Tour Trail
20. East Martello Tower Museum
21. Key West Lighthouse Museum
22. Fort Zachary Taylor
23. Fort Jefferson
24. Dry Tortugas
25. Southernmost Point
26. Mallory Docks Sunset

The Keys

The Keys gleam like gems set in a sea that dazzles from transparent turquoise and milky emerald to deep sapphire. Strung on a ribbon of concrete and steel better known as the **Overseas Highway,** this archipelago curves 100 miles from Biscayne Bay to Key West. Nearly 70 miles west of the highway's end in Key West are a few leftover jewels, which Ponce de Leon christened the Tortugas (Spanish for turtles).

These frostfree islands, warmed by the Gulf Stream in winter and cooled by the trade winds in summer, appear to be an uncomplicated antidote for the winter weary. Nothing in their swaying palms or glistening sandy beaches offers the slightest hint of a tempestuous past.

Yet early history of the Keys is peppered with both drama and tragedy. Ponce de Leon, who claimed Florida for Spain in 1513, charted the Keys and named them Los Martires (The Martyrs), because from a distance they looked like men who were suffering. The name proved to be prophetic. Spanish ships, laden with gold and treasures from Central America, were routinely plundered as they passed the islands. Such famous pirates as Black Caesar, Blackbeard and Lafitte found the Keys' many inlets and coves ideal for concealing their ships and stashing their booty.

By the turn of the century the Keys were more than ready for tycoon Henry Flagler's incredible scheme to link them to the mainland by rail. His idea was to extend his famous Florida East Coast Railroad across 100 miles of water and twenty-nine islands. As one of the founders of Standard Oil, Flagler had plenty of wealth to devote to this grand project popularly known as Flagler's Folly. At age seventy-five, having spent a lifetime responding to improbable challenges, he could afford to ignore those who said it couldn't be done. Besides, it didn't seem like such a big deal. "All you have to do," he said, "is to build one concrete arch, and then another, and pretty soon you will find yourself in Key West."

Unfortunately, the railroad turned out to be an economic failure. To make matters worse, a horrendous hurricane tore through the Keys in 1935 destroying embankments and even sweeping a train into the sea. After nearly two and one half years of relative isolation, the impoverished people of the Keys were delighted when the state of Florida built the 128-mile Overseas Highway. The highway, a continuation of U.S. 1, is an incredible engineering feat consisting of 113 miles of roadway and forty-three bridges.

Residents of the Keys, buoyed by their new accessibility, placed their hope for the future in tourism, a hope that has become reality. More than a million tourists each year seek out the Keys' subtropical climate and easy-going island lifestyle. They are usually in quest of an off-the-beaten-path experience, and they are rarely disappointed with what they find. You can traverse the highway in less than three hours, but then you can also see the Mona Lisa in less than a minute. The point is to take your time and enjoy. There are lots of things to see and do, but you will need to slow down to fully absorb and appreciate the natural beauty that surrounds you.

The Upper Keys, those nearest the mainland, stretch from Key Largo through Long Key. Key Largo is the base for the nation's first underwater park. **John Pennekamp Coral Reef State Park,** 21 miles long and approximately 4 miles wide, protects 40 species of coral and 650 species of fish on the only living reef along the Atlantic Coast. The reef, which was severely damaged by commercial souvenir hunters in the 1930s and 1940s, has recovered under the park's protection. These spectacular coral gardens were saved by a conservation movement spearheaded by John Pennekamp, an associate editor of the *Miami Herald,* whose stories fired up public interest in this national treasure.

Dive shops abound in Key Largo as do scuba diving courses culminating in certification. Skin divers, snorkelers and passengers on glass bottom boats revel in the park's clearwater views to 60 feet, which include colorful coral formations, exotic fish, turtles and old sailing wrecks. Christ of the Deep, a replica of Guido Galletti's *Christ of the Abyss* in the Mediterranean Sea, highlights one of the reef's natural underwater valleys.

The *M/V Discovery,* a glass bottom boat, leaves three times daily (9:00 A.M., noon and 3:00 P.M.) for a guided tour of Molasses Reef. You'll see high coral ridges, tunnels and a variety of formations including elkhorn, staghorn, star and brain coral without ever getting wet. Certified scuba divers may board *Dive Master,* a boat that leaves daily at 9:30 A.M. and 1:30 P.M. for trips to Molasses Reef, French Reef or Benwood Reef (depending on conditions). Snorkelers take advantage of a convenient dive platform on *El Capitan,* a boat which leaves three times daily on two-and-one half—hour reef trips. Usually the excursion heads for Grecian Rocks where you'll see colorful angelfish, parrotfish and some harmless nurse sharks.

John Pennekamp Park also has canoe, windsurfer and Hobie Cat rentals as well as beaches and nature trails. The campsites are much in demand so be sure to make reservations well ahead or get there early. John Pennekamp Coral Reef State Park, P. O. Box 487, Key Largo, FL 33037; (305) 451–1202.

At the Key Largo Holiday Inn you may see the ***African Queen,*** an old river freighter that Humphrey Bogart and Katharine Hepburn made famous in the 1951 film classic. The recently remodeled inn now has a Casa Blanca Lounge and Greenstreet's Restaurant.

Theatre of the Sea in Islamorada (Spanish for Purple Isle) is the second-oldest marine-life park in the world. A ninety-minute tour includes a look at an extensive shark and ray collection and a dolphin show in a natural coral grotto. Who knows? This may be your only chance to be kissed by an affectionate sea lion, touch a shark (and come away with all your fingers intact) or feed a stingray. For information and reservations on "Swim with a Dolphin" program, call (305) 664–2431. Open 9:30 A.M.—4:00 P.M. daily. Theatre of the Sea is on U.S. 1, P. O. Box 407, Islamorada, FL 33036; (305) 664–2431.

From Indian Key Fill on U.S. 1, you can take boat tours of both Lignumvitae Key and Indian Key. Boat tours leave for **Indian Key** State Historic Site at 8:30 A.M. and for **Lignumvitae Key** State Botanical Site at 1:30 P.M. Closed Tuesday and Wednesday. Lignumvitae was named for a type of hardwood tree with healing properties found growing here, and tours of the State Botanical Site reveal many other unusual plants. You'll be fascinated to learn how early Keys residents adapted the fruits, barks and leaves of the forest to meet their needs. Rangers say this nature preserve "is the last place which truly represents the Keys as they were."

A once-thriving settlement at Indian Key (a state historic site) was completely destroyed during the Seminole Indian raid in 1840. The tropical foliage here is amazing. Only at the top of the observation tower are you eye level with the tops of towering century plants. A marvelous time to visit is May when tiny white butterflies are migrating from South America. **Long Key State Park** is noted for great fishing, swimming, snorkeling, boating and camping. For information about the park and the boat tours to nearby keys, contact Park Manager, P. O. Box 776, Long Key, FL 33001; (305) 664-4815.

The Middle and Lower Keys (from Long Key on to Key West) differ geologically from the Upper Keys, which are the boney skeletons of an ancient coral reef. While all the islands have as a base a thick blanket of limestone, those farther from the mainland are topped with a layer of Miami oolite, egg-shaped particles cemented into rock by the millennium.

Each island seems to have a distinct identity, but most activities still center on Key favorites—beachcombing, sun basking and fishing from bridge, beach and boat. From Marathon to Key West, spearfishing is permitted one mile offshore. Marathon is the starting point for the famous **seven-mile bridge,** the country's longest continuous bridge. Its 65-foot crest is the highest point in the Keys.

Dainty Key Deer wander through the slash pines and mangrove swamps on Big Pine and a few surrounding Keys. This fragile subspecies, thought to have been stranded when the Wisconsin Glacier melted, is the smallest of all whitetail deer. From 26 to 32 inches in height, the deer average 38 inches in length and weigh between 30 and 110 pounds. By 1954 hunting and destruction of habitat had reduced the population of deer to fifty. The establishment of a **National Key Deer Refuge** protected the herd, which has stabilized at about 300. These deer, the size of a large dog, are still threatened with extinction primarily because of loss of habitat and ill-advised feeding by residents and visitors. Feeding can cause the deer to congregate and bring them in contact with such death traps as cars, canals, fences and dogs. It is now against the law to feed the deer.

National Key Deer Refuge is north of U.S. 1 on Key Deer Boulevard (SR 940). The refuge headquarters is on Watson

Boulevard, east of Key Deer Boulevard, on Big Pine Key. Best times to see deer are early morning, late afternoon and early evening. Blue Hole, a rock quarry with a mean old alligator guarding a sign that says "Please don't feed the alligators," is nearby. For information contact the Refuge Manager at (305) 872–2239.

Now here's a truly batty idea—a highrise for bats. This weather-beaten, 35-foot wooden tower was built to solve a problem. You see, Righter Clyde Perky wanted tourists to enjoy his guest cottages, restaurant and marina, but they were turned off by hordes of dive-bombing mosquitoes. Perky knew bats had a ravenous appetite for mosquitoes so he built them the most comfortable lodging he could think of and decorated it with sex-scented bat droppings imported from Texas. Unfortunately, the bats never got wind of the project (although the neighbors certainly did), and the tower remains uninhabited. Modern spraying techniques have largely done away with the mosquito problem, and who can say the tower isn't a success in its own right—after all, it has survived several hurricanes and is listed on the National Register of Historic Places. The **Perky Bat Tower** is near mile marker 17 on the Gulf side of U.S. 1 on Sugarloaf Key.

Key West Area

At the end of the Overseas Highway where the Atlantic meets the Gulf of Mexico is Key West, the southernmost city in the Continental United States. Here the Calusa Indians made a final stand against invading tribes from the north. The Spanish, who came upon the grisly remains of the battle, named it *Cayo Hueso,* which translates to the island of bones. Eventually this was anglicized into Key West.

Unruffled by the crosscurrents of its cultural heritage, this exotic community has long been a mecca for writers, artists and other well-knowns. The claim is that Key West is not really a place, but an attitude. The community's freewheeling spirit once led it to secede from the Union, establish the Conch Republic and demand foreign aid from the United States government! On this five-by-three mile island Ten-

Perky Bat Tower

nessee Williams spent the final years of his life, Harry Truman had his Little White House and John James Audubon painted tropical birds.

Stop in to visit the six-toed cats (direct descendants of those loved by "Papa" Hemingway) at the **Ernest Hemingway Home and Museum.** Hemingway bought this Spanish-Colonial—style house in 1931 and wrote a number of novels here. You'll see memorabilia, original furnishings and exotic trees and plants from around the world. Open daily 9:00 A.M.—5:00 P.M., 907 Whitehead Street, Key West, FL 33040; (305) 294–1575.

More Hemingway memorabilia is on tap at **Sloppy Joe's,** Papa's favorite bar at 201 Duval Street, Key West, FL 33040.

The **Audubon House** contains many of John J. Audubon's original engravings as well as a video about his life. Authentically restored with eighteenth- and nineteenth-century furnishings, this early nineteenth-century house is now a public museum. Once you've seen the incredible bird life on the Keys, it's not hard to understand why this famed naturalist-artist spent so much time here. The Audubon House is at 205 Whitehead Street at Green Street, Key West, FL 33040. Open daily 9:30 A.M.—5:00 P.M.; (305) 294–2116.

Visit the **Turtle Kralls** (*krall* is a Dutch/South African word originally meaning an enclosure for livestock) in the shrimp-dock area. The huge loggerhead turtles kept here weigh as much as 400 pounds. There is a touch tank for those who can't wait to get their hands on some ocean-going creatures. Free. The adjoining waterfront restaurant and bar, which open at noon daily, are at 2 Land's End Village, Key West, FL 33040; (305) 294–2640.

The **Mel Fisher Maritime Heritage Society Museum** has treasures recovered from Spanish galleons that have been slumbering on the ocean floor for centuries. Along with more than 150 pounds of gold are silver bullion, emeralds, diamonds, copper, brass cannons, rare antiques and a wonderful collection of historic artifacts. All told, the treasure, worth more than $40 million, is one of the largest displays of its type anywhere.

Feast your eyes on gold doubloons and discs, more than fifty gold bars and thirty-five gold chains—including one measuring 12 feet and weighing more than six pounds. The prize piece from the salvaged collection is a gold poison cup featuring a bezoar stone that changes color when it comes in contact with a toxic substance. You just can't be too careful! Mel Fisher's Gold Exhibit is at 200 Greene Street, Key West, FL 33040. Open 10:00 A.M.—6:00 P.M. daily; (305) 294–2633.

Once shipwrecks were the area's economic mainstay. Settlers from the mainland, the Bahamas and Europe flocked to the Keys to partake in the rich harvest of the sea. In 1825 Congress legislated that all salvage taken from wrecks in United States waters must be taken to a United States port for arbitration. Key West, as the islands' first permanent settlement, became the center for the auction of cargoes and repair of ships. By the 1830s wrecking had made Key West the wealthiest city, per capita, in the entire United States of America. The long dreary years of economic draught that followed were not endured in vain. Had the town enjoyed a history of uninterrupted prosperity rather than prolonged recession, its architectural treasure trove might have been leveled to make way for more modern buildings.

The **Wrecker's Museum** in the Oldest House in Key West is actually two houses, typical of 1830s "conch" construction. Browse the displays on the wrecking industry that once made Key West such a wealthy community. Don't miss the elegantly furnished dollhouse, the old kitchen house and large garden. Guided tours 10:00 A.M.—4:00 P.M. Maintained by the Old Island Restoration Foundation, 322 Duval Street, Key West, FL 33040; (305) 294–9502.

A massive restoration effort, centered in **Duval Street,** is currently saving classic buildings that infuse the city with its Old World air. The architecture is a melange of Bahaman, Spanish, New England and Southern styles. The Oldest House (circa 1829) in Key West is typical of small residences of that time. Many old homes were built in the 1850s by master ship carpenters who insisted on the best materials and used wooden pegs instead of nails. These handsome homes with wide verandas and gingerbread trim suggest a slower, more gracious era. Some of the most attractive, known as "Conch" houses, were built in sections in the Bahamas and shipped over on schooners.

If you can possibly schedule your visit to coincide with **Old Island Days,** which begin in January and end in March, do so. The residents of this small island community wear bright red and white to mark the festivities as the entire island celebrates its heritage with house and garden tours, food fests, plays, flower shows, sidewalk art festivals and even a conch shell blowing contest. For information contact Florida Keys and Key West Visitors Bureau, P.O. Box 1147, Key West, FL 33041; or call (305) 294–2587.

Natives of Key West are called Conchs (pronounced "konks") for the mollusk that thrives in local waters. This favorite local delicacy appears in chowders, fritters, in conch salad and as conch steak. Don't leave the islands without sampling stone crab, Florida lobster, shrimp and fresh-off-the-boat swordfish, yellowtail and red snapper. This is the perfect place to indulge in traditional Cuban dishes. Be sure to try a bowl of black bean soup and some bollos (pronounced bowyows), hush puppies made with mashed, shelled black-eyed peas instead of corn meal. For dessert, Key lime pie, made from piquant Key limes which flourish here, wins hands down.

Tourists who take the **Conch Tour Train,** an open-air tram, get a good look at the restoration area as well as the island's major points of interest. This one-and-a-half-hour tour promises "sixty of the most unusual historical sites you've ever seen." Boarding locations are Mallory Square and Roosevelt Avenue. 9:00 A.M.—4:00 P.M. daily. Contact Conch Tour Train at 601 Duval Street, Suite 8, P. O. Box 1173, Key West, FL 33040; (305) 294–5161.

History buffs will want to visit the **East Martello Tower Museum,** part of the nineteenth-century effort to fortify the country's southern boundary. Ground was broken for East Martello Tower in 1861, but the fort was never involved in a battle. A large collection of artifacts from the Keys (including implements used in cigar making and sponge diving) is housed in the fort's long series of casements, and two permanent art collections are on display. East Martello Gallery and Museum is adjacent to the airport at 3500 S. Roosevelt Boulevard, Key West, FL 33040. Open 9:30 A.M.—5:00 P.M. daily; (305) 296–3913.

You'll get a commanding view from the newly restored 110-foot tower of the lighthouse in the **Key West Lighthouse Museum.** Built in 1847, the museum pays tribute to the unique military history of the Florida Keys and contains many military artifacts. Open daily 9:30 A.M.—5:00 P.M. Key West Lighthouse Museum, 938 Whitehead Street, Key West, FL 33040; (305) 294–0012.

Key West's newest state park, dedicated on July 4, 1985, is **Fort Zachary Taylor.** This pre–Civil War fortress is a reminder of a time when Union troops occupied Key West during the Civil War. To uncover Fort Taylor's mysteries, Howard England worked alone for nine years with bucket and shovel to uncover the country's largest known collection of Civil War cannons. He assembled a small museum with artifacts, photographs and a model of the original fort. The park, with one of the finest natural beaches on the island, is an ideal spot to swim and picnic. Open 8:00 A.M.—sunset every day. Write c/o Bahia Honda State Recreation Area, Rte. 1, Box 782, Big Pine Key, FL 33043. For information: 1–800–FLA–KEYS.

At Key West arrangements can be made to fly 68 miles west to **Fort Jefferson,** a National Monument in the Dry Tortugas. The low-flying seaplane passes over shifting sandbars, clearly identifiable sharks and an old Spanish wreck that has coughed up millions of dollars worth of treasure. Passengers look down on the Marquesas, a ring of islands considered by some to be the only atoll in the Atlantic Ocean.

The Tortugas were considered of great strategic importance to the United States. Because the U.S. War Department believed the nation that occupied these islands could protect navigation in the Gulf, it decided to fortify them. Construction began on Fort Jefferson in 1846. Complete with 50-foot high walls and water-filled moat, the hexagonal fort covered most of 16-acre Garden Key. It was to be the strongest link in the chain of coastal forts that reached from Maine to Texas during the first half of the 1800s.

Federal troops occupied Fort Jefferson throughout the Civil War but saw little action. Although work continued on the fort for thirty years, it was never completed primarily because the new rifled cannon introduced during the war had already made it obsolete. Used as a military stronghold for captured deserters during the Civil War, Fort Jefferson continued as a prison for almost ten years after the fighting had ceased.

The fort's most famous prisoner was Dr. Samuel Mudd, the

physician who set John Wilkes Booth's broken leg after Booth assassinated Abraham Lincoln. Brought here in 1865 and sentenced to a lifetime of hard labor, he earned an early pardon by tirelessly tending victims of a yellow fever epidemic that swept through the fort. Be sure to see the orientation slide program before taking the self-guiding tour.

Snorkeling is especially good off the moat walls of Fort Jefferson. Coral formations and brilliant tropical fish provide fine opportunities for underwater photography. Saltwater fishing is good most of the year and no fishing license is required.

Fort Jefferson is open during daylight hours only. Public transportation to the fort is available from Key West by seaplane. Those who want to go by private boat may purchase nautical charts at marinas and boating supply outlets in Key West. Boaters should be aware of the possibility of extremely rough seas. The Tortugas are isolated, and you must provide for yourself. No housing, water, meals or supplies are available. Camping is permitted in the grassed picnic area. For more information, write the Superintendent of Everglades National Park, Box 279, Homestead, FL 33030; (305) 247–6211. For information on charter boats and flights, contact the Greater Key West Chamber of Commerce, 402 Wall Street, Old Mallory Square, Key West, FL 33040; (305) 294–2587.

Frigate birds with seven-foot wingspans soar above the cerulean waters surrounding the **Dry Tortugas.** Sooty terns, which have turned Bush Key into a rookery, lay their eggs in shallow depressions on its warm sandy beaches. The Tortugas also host noddy terns, brown and blue-faced boobies and a variety of passing songbirds en route from Cuba and South America. During the nesting season from March to September, Bush Key is reserved for birds only. All keys, other than Garden Key and Loggerhead Key, are closed during the turtle season from May through the end of September.

Visitors should not leave Key West without seeing the **Southernmost Point** in the continental United States. (The Big Island of Hawaii claims the honor for the nation.) Chinese immigrant Jim Kee began selling shells here in the late 1930s and his descendants still cater to tourists' yen for souvenirs.

Some of Key West's appeal is its temperature, which varies

only twelve degrees and averages a balmy 77, and some is its luxuriant palms, hibiscus, oleander, bougainvillaea and fragrant frangipani blooms. But the city's greatest charm is that it is a true original.

Few other communities have the good sense to elaborate such a daily marvel as the sunset. The crowd starts to gather at **Mallory Docks** about a half an hour before the main event. The Cookie Lady arrives on her bicycle and does a bustling business selling warm brownies and cookies. Locals show off their parrots and pet iguanas. Some juggle, dance, sing or swallow flaming swords. All the entertainment is free (although the entertainers do pass a hat). After the sun's final farewell, everyone heartily applauds the performance.

For those who have purposely strayed far from the beaten path, it is an entirely appropriate celebration—a fine way to end a day or, for that matter, a book.

Acknowledgments

Our thanks to the Florida Division of Tourism, especially Sally Lane, Greg Yon, Jan Tully, Poppy Rittwage, and Dixie Lee Nims.

Also, a round of grateful applause to Bill Hensley, Mac Seligman, Stu Newman, Susan Maass, Nancy House, Beth Sullivan, Beth Walters, Gary Stogner, Laura Davidson, Margaret Goff Clark, Virginia Vidler, Pegi Adam, Joice Veselka, Gary LaBella, and Elizabeth Cottle.

About the Authors

Diana and Bill Gleasner, an award-winning writer/photographer team, have thirty published books to their credit as well as hundreds of articles for national and international magazines and newspapers. As professional travel photojournalists who have roamed the globe in search of fascinating travel experiences, they admit a continuing addiction to Florida. The Gleasners are members of the Society of American Travel Writers, Travel Journalists Guild, American Society of Magazine Photographers, and the American Society of Journalists and Authors.

Index

135